History of a Tragedy

Hispanisms

Series Editor
Anne J. Cruz

*A list of books in the series appears
at the back of this book.*

History of a Tragedy

The Expulsion of the Jews from Spain

Joseph Pérez

Translated from the Spanish by Lysa Hochroth

Introduction by Helen Nader

University of Illinois Press

Urbana and Chicago

English translation © 2007 by the Board of Trustees
of the University of Illinois

Publication of this book was supported by a grant from the
Joseph and Harvey Meyerhoff Family Charitable Funds.

Historia de una tragedia: La expulsión de los Judíos de España
© 1993 by Joseph Pérez.
Reprinted by arrangement with the proprietor.
Manufactured in the United States of America
C 5 4 3 2 1

∞ This book is printed on acid-free paper.

Library of Congress Cataloging-in-Publication Data
Peréz, Joseph.
[Historia de una tragedia. English]
History of a tragedy : the expulsion of the Jews from Spain / Joseph Peréz ;
translated from the Spanish by Lysa Hochroth ; introduction by Helen Nader.
p.   cm. — (Hispanisms)
Includes bibliographical references and index.
ISBN-13: 978–0–252–03141–0 (cloth : alk. paper)
ISBN-10: 0–252–03141–5 (cloth : alk. paper)
1. Jews—Spain—History. 2. Spain—Ethnic relations. 3. Civilization, Medieval—
Jewish influences.
I. Hochroth, Lysa. II. Title.
DS135.S7P39813   2007
946'.004924—dc22   2006036185

Contents

Translator's Preface: A Case Study in the Limits of Tolerance and Assimilation

Lysa Hochroth

When Joseph Pérez describes the expulsion of the Jews from Spain as the result of Spain shedding its medieval heterogeneity in order to join the ranks of other powerful Christian European nations, we realize the importance of understanding the limits of tolerance and assimilation in European history. If absolute royal power had to be founded on the religious, political, and ideological identification between rulers and subjects, it is logical that such power could only successfully be established by excluding medieval society's nonhomogeneous elements (Jews, Muslims, pagans, heretics, and other refuseniks). As Pérez and others have emphasized, Spain was the last European nation to expel Jews, a continental conclusion that was, as it turned out, a necessary prerequisite for New World expansionism.

After almost a millennium of varying degrees of tolerating Jewish religious practices and self-government, neither assimilation, whether through forced or voluntary mass conversions to Christianity, especially after the anti-Jewish violence of 1391, or integrating some prominent Jews to positions of power by rulers in Spain made the difficult cohabitation between Christians and Jews anything more than provisional. Tolerance definitively ended once the idea of national sovereignty, the basis for territorial hegemony and absolute rule, reached the mimetic plateau of subjects having to espouse the same religion as their sovereigns (*cujus regio ejus religio*).

Tolerance must be understood as a temporary and therefore inherently reversible attitude. Assimilation, produced by religious conversions, the progeny of mixed marriages, or even certain contemporary ideas of citizenship, tends to neutralize differences and assume the necessity of embracing at least the outward appearances of the more powerful majority affiliation. In times of crisis, however, whatever the cause, tolerance seems reversed and the politics of exclusion begin. The failure to complete assimilation and the insincerity of the conversion are used as pretexts for putting an end to a paternalistic attitude of acquiescence on the part of those in power who claim or insinuate the inferiority and subservient status of those being tolerated. The law in its most evolved form of the day (in the late fifteenth century, edicts or decrees, accusations, arrests, trials, and sentences) is then used to justify politically the necessary exclusions in order to consolidate a newly reconquered power.

In translating this history, certain terms foreign to the Spanish language yet integrated into usage took on special and extended meanings, a linguistic phenomenon mirroring the political logic of expansionism in 1492. Examples include terms from Arabic such as *aljama* (originally, an assembly of Moslems in a mosque or Jews in a synagogue), which was extended in use to refer specifically to Jews' separatist self-governing assemblies and courts, and *dhimma* (the Islamic designation for the protection of minority status), which evolved into a way to refer to Jews' privileged status in Christian Spain, where they were specially protected vassals and subjects of the monarch. From Latin, the Papal Inquisition's original target, *pravitas heretica* (heretical depravity in all forms of non-Catholic anti-Papism), was extended to Jews under the Spanish Inquisition, and, finally, *universitas* (a community of any kind or group of people practicing the same trade) was ultimately expanded to define minority religious communities such as Jews and false converts who threatened the Christian res publica.

The emergence of the Catholic Spanish national identity depended on repossessing territories under Moorish rule and eliminating the remaining unconverted Jews and false converts on these lands. That was achieved by expanding jurisdictions. The "Reconquista" was a holy war crusade against the Moors, and the Spanish Inquisition, originally used only to persecute heretics and false converts, expanded and became nationalized to enforce the expulsion of the Jewish population. Torquemada, the inquisitor general for the Inquisition, an appointee of Ferdinand and Isabel and not the pope, was able to devise the necessary logic in his edict of 1492. Eradicating the remaining false converts (and the preservation of Christianity from pravitas heretica) remained impossible as long as Jews continued to cohabit and communicate with converted Christians (i.e., former Jews), which unduly influenced and contaminated them, inciting them to continue Jewish practices in secret (*judaizing*). Torquemada was thus able to establish the legal (inquisitorial) justification for physically removing Jews from Spain by citing exposure to Jews as a danger to Christians' health and well-being.

Although it was recognized that few Jews were guilty of proselytism, in the greater interest of the Christian Spanish nation the community as a whole (*universitas*) had to be held responsible for the misconduct of its members and punished collectively by being dissolved. This point in history serves as a lesson regarding the bases for the alternating practices of tolerance and exclusion because it concurrently illustrates the foundations of European jurisprudence and legal principles such as guilt by association. There is no doubt that the imposition of religious homogeneity created absolute rule and a sense of national identity in Europe.

Despite the French Revolution and the European Union, today's Europe still suffers from this legacy through the resurgence of nationalism, racism, and fascism. The present relevance of Pérez's text is that the underlying juridical foundations of European states remain weak barriers for excessive oscillations between protecting and scape-goating. Namely, the separation of church and state is ill-defined when a perceived national interest is at stake. States can approve or disapprove plans to build places of worship, rule on dress codes for public schools to prevent religious "ostentatiousness," amend immigration policies to suit, and use state budgets to support churches and their properties. Likewise, given the ruling powers' ability to rewrite constitutions, issue new and substantially contradictory laws, and reinaugurate republics by changing the political parties in power, governments' role in protecting minority rights and those of noncitizens is as ill-conceived as the concept of tolerance. The mimetic plateau in European states where the monarchy remains an ideal symbol of power despite parliamentary governments is frozen in an image of a certain kind of religion; culture and national identity is reflected in royals always being in church, whether at weddings or funerals.

How can new immigrants in Western Europe assimilate or integrate when models are based on unattainable appearances? As archaic as organized religion remains today, the repression of religious practices has all too often proven to have a backlash, and it increases orthodoxy and fundamentalism, especially for those who confuse religion with politics (more often than not, state politics).

Christopher Columbus departed from Spain on August 3, 1492, on a fleet of three ships: the *Niña*, the *Pinta*, and the *Santa Maria*. *Niña* and *Pinta* were both smaller, sleeker ships, called caravels. *Santa Maria* was a larger, round-hulled ship, called a *nao*. Columbus himself sailed aboard, and piloted, the *Santa Maria*. It is no coincidence that the voyage began on the very day of the expulsion deadline. Together, the three ships carried about 120 men as well as equipment and supplies. Perhaps, as financing for the voyage and a missing page of Columbus's log seem to suggest, the expedition was a charter for Jews and converts who sought asylum at sea. Yet the true irony of the exponential expansionism of European Christianity was that in the Americas—where so many indigenous civilizations were summarily destroyed in the name of the Crown and Christianity—it was possible to expand the idea of the French Revolution and, through the American experiment, lay a foundation for basing a society on the equality of individual rights: freedom of religion, speech, and assembly.

It is well worth recalling, especially in time of crisis, whatever its cause, that freedom of expression is the best safeguard in countering fanaticism. That freedom (not obligation) includes exhibiting outward signs of belonging to a religious, ethnic, political, or cultural community in the context of a secular state wherein the division of church and state is demonstrated by protecting the rights of minorities to affirm their differences. Nothing is as beneficially contagious as the freedom to express oneself.

Introduction

Helen Nader

In 1492 Fernando, king of Aragon, and his wife, Isabel, queen of Castile, expelled the Jews from their respective kingdoms. That expulsion lingers in communal memory as one of the worst tragedies of European history. Thousands of Spanish Jews converted to Christianity and remained in Castile and Aragon. Most of those who did not convert in 1492 traveled by land to the neighboring kingdoms of Navarre and Portugal, only to convert to Christianity and return to Spain within about five years. Some of the wealthiest and most prominent Jewish leaders and their extended families took ship to North Africa, Italy, and the Ottoman Empire, where they retained their religion and identity as Jews.

For Spain, the consequences of the expulsion have been a matter of heated debate. Ardent admirers of Queen Isabel regard her actions as wise and necessary; they believe that the continued presence of Jewish communities in Castile's cities undermined the religious unity of the monarchy and disrupted the peace and tranquility of urban politics. Historians with more secular interests have argued that, by expelling the Jews, Queen Isabel irreparably damaged the Castilian economy, driving out the most expert and successful businessmen and bankers and leaving the kingdom bereft of financial skills. Ultimately, they believe, the expulsion led to a weakening of Spain's economic and military strength and, consequently, to the decline of Spain in the seventeenth century.

For the Spanish Jews (Sephardim) and their descendants, the expulsion was an unmitigated disaster and one that throughout the centuries has carried a powerful emotive charge. Traditionally, Jewish historians have painted preexpulsion Jewish society as a vibrant, prosperous, and creative community. Jewish poets, theologians, doctors, and financiers enjoyed the respect of all three cultures—Christian, Jewish, and Muslim—in a Spain of peaceful coexistence. That view was popularized by the Spanish lexicographer Américo Castro, who coined the term *convivencia* to describe the peaceful cohabitation that he believed prevailed among the three cultures.[1] Castro's much-quoted statements have given substance to a powerful sense of homesickness that many Jewish authors project when describing preexpulsion Jewish culture in the Iberian Peninsula. They look back on convivencia as a golden age in Jewish History, a period of intellectual vitality and peaceful coexistence unique in medieval Europe and not matched again until modern times.

Only recently has this widespread consensus about convivencia come under scholarly scrutiny. Medieval historian Jocelyn Hillgarth challenged the idea of a peaceful coexistence among the three faiths; he argued instead that distrust, prejudice, and conflict permeated the relationships among the three cultures.[2] And that revision has been given flesh and blood in the description of Jewish and Christian social relationships described by David Nirenberg.[3] Rather than convivencia, these historians see a society that managed to survive and be creative despite simmering and frequently overt hostility. Thus the expulsion ended not a golden age but a barely tolerable state of tension and prejudice.

Into this variety of interpretations, Joseph Pérez brings a broad understanding of medieval European Jewry. He emphasizes that Spain was the last European nation to expel its Jews, and he explains the expulsion of the Jews from Spain as the result of Spain's shedding its medieval heterogeneity in order to catch up with other powerful Christian European nations that had already achieved homogeneous societies through expulsions. The Spanish expulsion not only occurred very late compared to other countries but also in a more humane manner. In France, the expulsion was carried out in the typical manner for medieval Europe. King Philip the Fair in 1306 decreed that "every Jew must leave my land." For months in strict secrecy he had been planning how and when the expulsion would be done. He ordered local magistrates to count and name the Jews in their territories, set a specific date for the magistrates to seize the Jews and their property, and designated locations where the Jews were to be collected. On the scheduled night, all the Jews in France were seized, and within twenty-four hours they were conducted to collection points, from whence they were forced to walk to the borders of France, regardless of their physical condition.[4] In Spain, in contrast, Fernando and Isabel in January 1492 set a deadline of March (later extended to August) to give the Jews time to convert (an option not permitted in the French case) or to sell their property and make travel arrangements. Thus, from the beginning, Joseph Pérez alerts us to the surprises, the new discoveries, and the changing interpretations that we will encounter throughout the book. For Pérez, the question of anti-Semitism is not a Spanish problem but a European one.

In this book, Joseph Pérez gives us an overview drawing together recent research by historians of all traditions. He discerns that any interpretation of the expulsion and its consequences must necessarily grow out of an interpretation of the history of Jews in medieval Spain. We cannot know the origins and consequences of the tragedy, he argues, unless we have a broad and detailed knowledge of the Jews and their situation before 1492—the very subject on which historians have been focusing their research since the 1980s. Pérez, therefore, masterfully leads us on a tour through the lives, occupations, demographics, and travails of medieval Spanish Jews. Along the way, several icons in traditional interpretations fall by the wayside. New evidence discovered by recent researchers disproves some of the most hallowed assumptions, and old evidence is now shown to have been incorrectly interpreted. Readers, therefore, must be prepared to find some of their most basic beliefs challenged and to discover new compassion and admiration for the victims of this tragic event.

Joseph Pérez focuses his interpretation on two major issues: the reasons for and consequences of the expulsion from Spain in 1492. He emphasizes that royal protection of the Jews could be maintained only in conditions of economic expansion and political stability. By 1492, the medieval climate of stability had long been disrupted. In 1475 the Kingdom of Castile plunged into turmoil, providing ripe conditions for a drastic and worsening change in the relationship between the monarchy and its non-Christian subjects. Isabel of Castile, recently proclaimed queen of Castile after the death of her half-brother King Enrique IV, called a meeting of Castile's parliament, the Cortes. At the Cortes meeting in the town of Madrigal on April 27, 1476, Isabel and her husband Fernando, then heir to the throne of Aragon, asked the delegates to levy a special tax in order to fund wars against the Portuguese king, who had invaded Castile intending to depose Isabel and replace her with Juana, the infant daughter of Enrique IV. The city delegates to the Cortes, in exchange for taxes, asked the young monarchs to approve forty-four petitions on a wide range of subjects. That Fernando and Isabel agreed to all the requests, without amendment, indicates the desperation of their political situation.

Traditionally, Spanish kings had protected and even favored their Jewish and Muslim subjects against popular hostility; a weak or contested monarchy, therefore, created a perilous climate for Castile's religious minorities. Five of the forty-four petitions from the Cortes of Madrigal asked the monarchs to limit the freedoms and privileges of non-Christians. The delegates asked the monarchs to revoke centuries-old laws that exempted Jews and Muslims from imprisonment for debt to a Christian.[5] The delegates also asked that Fernando and Isabel prohibit Jews and Muslims from wearing silk or red clothing or displaying gold or silver on their saddles or spurs. They further demanded that Jews must wear a blue patch on the right shoulder and Muslims must wear a green patch or capelet over their clothing.[6] The monarchs also agreed without a murmur to revoke the power they and their predecessors had given to Jewish and Muslim judges in allowing them to hold jurisdiction in criminal cases; from now on, these judges were limited to civil cases.[7] The delegates expressed their hostility and prejudices most sharply in their petition that the king and queen prohibit Jews and Muslims from making fraudulent credit contracts by writing contracts for less than they intended to collect or by falsifying a contract already written.[8]

These measures against non-Christians were part of a larger, more pervasive resentment against the "others" in Castilian society. In the same Cortes, the delegates asked Fernando and Isabel to revoke letters of naturalization granted to Italians and to other foreign clergy who held benefices in the kingdom.[9] The climate of economic expansion and political stability, which Joseph Pérez emphasizes was necessary for the well-being of Jews, had evaporated in the succession crisis (ch. 2).

Year by year, Fernando and Isabel's policy became harsher. Jews had always lived where they chose in Spanish cities and towns; there were no ghettos in medieval Spain. In 1480, however, Queen Isabel ordered all Jews to move into designated neighborhoods of their home cities, and she instructed each city to erect walls around these newly formed ghettos. When Fernando and Isabel conquered the Muslim city of Málaga in 1487 they enslaved all the inhabitants, including six thousand Jews, whereas royal practice during the medieval Reconquest had been to incorporate defeated Muslims and Jews into the newly formed Christian city. Finally, within twenty years of the Cortes of Madrigal, Isabel and Fernando (who had succeeded his father as king of Aragon in 1479), ordered all Jews, and another ten years later all Muslims, to convert to Christianity or leave Spain.

The departure of the Jews led to several consequences whose scope and significance are still hotly debated. For Joseph Pérez, these results can only be evaluated in light of what the Jews themselves had contributed to Spanish society and to what degree those contributions were distinctively or even exclusively Jewish in nature. On this issue Pérez departs decisively from other interpretations. He rejects out of hand the notion of three cultures. He maintains that "Jews adopted the language and culture of the society in which they lived: first the Moslem and then the Christian." As a result, "It is still not possible to speak of a strictly Jewish culture in an absolute sense" (27). Nor did the Jews live in a peaceful and tolerant atmosphere. At times of expansion such as the twelfth and thirteenth centuries, they experienced an extended period of progress and prosperity, whether in Muslim or Christian kingdoms. "That [period] was later idealized and turned into the myth of the existence of three cultures, medieval pluralism, and the Golden Age of Spanish Judaism. Nonetheless, no such pluralism actually existed; in fact, Jews were simply tolerated" (31).[10]

Pérez turns his guns on other aspects of the consequences, reinterpreting the comparative skills of Jews and Christians. He presents a quantity of evidence to demolish one of Américo Castro's most popular claims, that Christians lacked the ability to work in the crafts or in business. Thus, whatever may have caused the decline of Spain, it was not because Spanish Christians could not function productively and economically. They had always worked as craftsmen and financiers and continued to do so after 1492.

With so many assumptions and interpretations now buried under the weight of evidence researched by many scholars and presented here in brief by Joseph Pérez, a new understanding of the tragedy of the expulsion should soon emerge. Readers will find much to absorb or reject in Pérez's interpretations. At the same time, they may find in the abundant evidence presented here fortification for their personal beliefs or the building blocks for constructing their own interpretations.

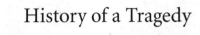History of a Tragedy

Preface

The year 1492 is known in the history of Spain for three decisive events: the capture of Granada, Santa Fe's capitulations authorizing Christopher Columbus to undertake his voyage to the West, and the expulsion of the Jews. The latter two events are those which have given rise to the most controversy and debate and yet are nonetheless a direct consequence of the first. The euphoric mood at the end of the Reconquest explains how it came to pass that the Catholic monarchs had ultimately accepted the seemingly absurd and utopian project of discovery. Spain was feeling confident in itself, confident enough to indulge in this type of fantasy. The expulsion of the Jews was part and parcel of the same mood but in a much more concrete way. It was in fact the denouement of a long period of battles after so many centuries of more or less forced cohabitation between different religions. Victory over Islam allowed Spain to definitively incorporate itself into European Christianity and become a nation like other European nations, a Catholic country without Moors or Jews.

In recent years, since the fifth centennial anniversary of 1492, there have been serious and objective studies available on the last war of Granada. Although much debate continues to surround the discovery of America, or rather the consequences of the discovery, the expulsion of the Jews continues to be the most discussed decision. I was just reading that in Mexico a novel has been written attempting to reconstruct the historical, social, and ideological panorama of Spain in 1492: the intolerance, fanaticism, barbarism, the backdrop of the Inquisition, tortures, autos-da-fé—all naturally culminating in the expulsion of the Jews. This is only one example of a widespread contention that the Catholic monarchs' decision was a barbaric act of anti-Semitic phobia if not accused of even worse, a genocide comparable to the Holocaust waged by the Nazis during World War II.[1]

Why this ferocity against Spain and its sovereigns? Some Spaniards are in part responsible for this partial and partisan focus by insisting so much on the uniqueness of their nation within the European whole as if circumstances in Spain had nothing at all to do with those in the rest of Europe. Spain, like all nations, has its own particularities but not to the point of constituting a separate and independent entity. As far as anti-Semitism is concerned, it is by no means a Spanish monopoly. It developed throughout Europe, embodying practically the same forms, including expulsion, during approximately the same years. This leads us to think that it had similar causes in different areas.

If something distinguishes the case of Spain it is the late date at which the expulsion of its Jews took place. The Jews had been banished from England in 1290; France contemplated the same action in 1306 but held off until 1394. Throughout the entire fifteenth century, decisions of this sort were repeatedly made: in 1421, the Jews were expelled from Vienna, then from Linz, Cologne (1424), Augsburg (1439), Bavaria (1442), Perugia (1485), Vicenza (1486), Parma (1488), and from Milan and Lucca (1489). A few years later they were in like manner expelled from Sicily (1493), Florence (1494), Provence (1498), Geneva, Magdeburg, and Ulm. By the beginning of the sixteenth century, Jews were not officially authorized to live in Western Europe, with the sole exception of the territories under papal authority. If something was peculiar then, it was not so much the Catholic monarchs' decision to expel the Jews from Spain at the end of the fifteenth century but the near total unanimity on the part of the European sovereigns to adopt this same position.[2]

How can we explain such rare unanimity in acting against Judaism? It occurred most probably because anti-Semitism was nourished on the same diet throughout Europe. The word itself is of recent origin. The adjective *Semite* appeared for the first time in 1781, penned by the German philosopher August Ludwig Schlözer, who used a neologism to designate a group of related languages: Hebrew, Aramaic, Arabic, and an Ethiopian idiom. In the mid-nineteenth century the term *Semitic race* began to be used generally in opposition to the Indo-European or Aryan race, and on specific occasions the term was used in a pejorative manner. The French philosopher and historian Ernest Renan (1823–92) used it in such a way, considering Semites inferior to Aryans. This led him to write of *de-Semitizing* Christianity, which he felt would then antonomastically become the equivalent to the Aryan religion. Building upon these ideas, in 1879 the German Wilhelm Marr created an anti-Semitic league, and contemporary anti-Semitism was born.

If the term is recent and refers to a specific historical context in which racist theories gained momentum throughout Europe, however, the concept is ancient, and to date no satisfactory explanation of its genesis and development exists. There is no doubt that its origin is religious. From its inception, Christianity, attempting to unite the legacy of the Bible with that of Hebraic monotheism, considered that Jesus Christ had fulfilled all the promises made to Abraham. Consequently, it held that Judaism, as such, no longer had reason to exist. Only the blindness and obstinacy of the rabbis could explain the continuity of such a religion. The Church's interpretation of the death of Christ must be added to this schema. As constant Church teaching upholds, Jews were unanimously condemned as the ones who obliged the Roman prelate Pilate to crucify Jesus and pronounce the horrible phrase in which the fate of the Jewish people was inscribed: "That his blood fall on us and on our children." For the Church, Jews were, from the beginning, the deicidal people who put Jesus to death. For centuries the Christian faithful heard nothing else about them in sermons or read anything but this interpretation in catechisms or scholarly or popular books. In fact, only since Vatican Council II has the Church accepted to soften the wording of this collective condemnation. This change began with Jules Isaac, a French professor of history and also a Jew, who produced a new in-depth interpretation of early Christian history that was written during the tragic period from 1940 to 1944 when the Vichy government was turning Jews over to the German police to be sent to crematoria. Due to Isaac's extensive efforts the highest Roman authorities were persuaded that decisive changes had to be made in the liturgy and cathechesis.

Until the 1970s, therefore, the Catholic Church continued to teach that the Jews constituted an evil people and that they, or at least their ancestors, were to bear the blame for the death of Christ. It is, however, useful to distinguish between doctrinal anti-Semitism and popular anti-Semitism. The Church cannot be held responsible for persecutions and killings committed by the common people. It is nonetheless difficult to excuse the Church for teaching the explanation that the populace has, century after century, heard that Jews were an evil race and then separate it from the results of these teachings. By encouraging Christians to regard Jews as deicidal, disloyal, and untrustworthy hardheads to be avoided, the Church laid the ground for all types of reactions, including the most violent. It was logical for Jews to be represented as a strange and malicious people who had put Jesus Christ to death and thus capable of anything. During periods of prosperity and general well-being, nothing much happened. But in times of crisis it was tempting to blame the Jews for all sorts of difficulties and, inasmuch as the circumstances warranted it, to take vengeance against those presumed to be responsible.

The Jews reacted by closing themselves off within their particularism and refusing to renounce what they considered to be the only revealed religion. In addition, until the nineteenth century there was no concept of secularism or religious neutrality within the state.[3] In truth, all the Western states during the Middle Ages considered that the sole solution to the Jewish problem was the disappearance of Judaism, the assimilation of the Jews and their conversion to Christianity. The sovereigns and social and intellectual elites were not racist; they knew Jews were not a separate, evil race. The masses, however, wound up being racist.

If this is the case, why is there still such indignation at the Catholic monarchs' decision of 1492? Surely it is connected to the fact that following the expulsions decreed in England and France at the end of the thirteenth and fourteenth centuries the Jewish community in Spain at the end of the fifteenth century was the most populous in Western Europe.

The aim of this book is to understand how and why Spain came to the conclusion that it too had to prohibit Judaism. It is in no way a means of justifying a measure that is entirely unacceptable given today's way of thinking. Rather, it is an attempt to show that Spain in 1492, in this specific case as in others, unfortunately constituted no exception to the family of nations that came to be involved in writing universal history.

1
The Jews in Medieval Spain

The Jewish presence on the Iberian peninsula is probably very ancient, although not as ancient as some later traditions would have it, because the first settlements apparently do not date quite as far back as the destruction of the first temple of Jerusalem (587 B.C.E.). This particular legend surfaced some time during the tenth century to demonstrate that although the Sephardi—that is, the Jews of Spain—descended from the tribe of Judas and therefore possessed a superior cultural level, they could in no way be held responsible for the trial and death of Jesus.[1] In fact, precise and reliable dates about the arrival of Jews in Iberia are lacking. Nonetheless, evidence seems to indicate that the first fairly significant groups arrived on the peninsula after the destruction of the second temple (70 C.E.). We have better documentation for the era of Roman rule.

Discussions and polemics about Christians who judaized when they came in contact with Jewish elements appeared during the Council of Elvira (Iliberis) at the beginning of the fourth century.[2] Texts of this period suggest that there were already Jewish communities in Catalonia; on the Balearic Islands; and in the Levant, Bética, and some inland areas (Avila, Astorga, and Mérida).[3] The bishops gathered at the council evidently worried about the Israelites' proselytism and were determined to separate these people from Christians.[4]

A similar geographical distribution of Jews can be observed after the fall of the Roman Empire and during the era of the Visigothic monarchy. There is documentation attesting to the presence of Jews in the coastal Mediterranean area (Barcelona, Tarragona, Tortosa, the Balearic Islands, Orihuela, and Elche); in the Guadalquivir Valley; in Granada; and near the center of the country, Toledo and Mérida. It is, however, difficult to estimate the numerical importance of the Jewish population at this time. What instead appears clear is that Jews did not constitute a distinct ethnic group; they were distinguished by their religious condition rather than as a separate race. Apart from their religious beliefs and certain customs related to them (such as celebrating the Sabbath on Saturdays and abstinence from certain types of foods), nothing differentiated Jews from the rest of the peninsula's Hispano-Roman population. The polemic concerning the Jews' eager proselytizing also indicates that in addition to the influx of Diaspora Jews from Palestine there were many peninsular converts. Mixed marriages were common, and these suggest that Spanish Jews of this period constituted a religious, not ethnic, minority. This important point dramatizes even further the expulsion of 1492 because Jews were used to considering themselves as Spanish as the old Christians. Having lived on the peninsula for centuries, they considered it their country, the land of their fathers and their ancestors.

Moreover, Jews did not constitute a separate social class. There were rich Jews, poor Jews, and those in between. Likewise, there was no profession exclusively exercised by Jews. Some were merchants although there is no indication that Jews demonstrated a pronounced preference for financial affairs. Documents of the period do not allude to Jewish usury as would be the case in later periods. From other sources we also know that much acquired land was cultivated by slaves and serfs. The professional repertoire of Jews was as broad and varied as any other social group. Apart from their religion, nothing distinguished them from the rest of the population.

The Jews in Visigothic Spain

Religion was precisely what unleashed the persecution of the Jews. In this case the dates are significant. All historians agree in pinpointing the change produced by conversion of King Recared to Roman Catholicism (ratified by the Third Council of Toledo in 589). Before this date, although there were a few measures remaining from the Roman period, these were apparently not enforced very strictly. This is true, for example, with regard to the Code of Alaric, which includes the old prohibition against Jews owning Christian slaves; it also attempted to halt Jewish proselytizing among Christians and limited the construction of new synagogues. Otherwise, the code allowed Jews to rebuild existing synagogues. It also gave them the right to judge grievances in their own courts, including civil matters, providing that both parties were Jews and had agreed upon it. In many ways this situation is reminiscent of the Roman Empire. The Visigothic monarchs, in this instance, limited themselves to maintaining existing legislation.

The first Visigoths were Arian Christians. As such, they constituted a dominant minority, exercising authority over this Hispano-Roman population, most of which professed Roman Catholicism. Anxious to achieve religious unity as well as territorial and juridical unity, the kings clashed with these masses. When Recared succeeded his father Leovigild in 586, he believed that he could solve these problems by converting to Roman Catholicism. From this moment on, the position of the Jews, the only dissident religious minority in an officially Catholic kingdom, changed. Recared initiated a discriminatory policy, implementing existing laws such as the one prohibiting Jews from owning Christian slaves, and then added others, notably a ban on mixed (i.e., Judeo-Christian) marriages, and excluded Jews from public office.

It was, however, King Sisebut (crowned in 612) who truly began the persecutions of Jews. He reiterated Recared's measures but extended them to include those Jews who had converted to Christianity and especially those suspected of practicing their former religion of Judaism in secret (crypto-Judaism). He also attempted to require Jews to convert to Catholicism, essentially by giving them a choice between exile and conversion. In addition, both converts and Jews were excluded from public office, apparently on the grounds that it was intolerable for them to have authority over Catholics.

By approximately 638, King Chintila had become even more discriminatory; what he wanted more than anything was for all his subjects to be Catholics. During the second half of the seventh century official violence against Jews reached its peak with the advent of death sentences by stoning and burning and with the establishment of certain restrictive laws that anticipated modern ethnic cleansing practices to "purify blood" in later epochs. When King Egica (610–701) came to power, he ordered nothing less than the enslavement of both Jews and converts.

How can one explain the fury of Spain's Visigothic monarchs, starting with Recared's conversion, when Jews as such did not constitute much of a threat? Explanations based on economic or political motivations are pointless; greediness does not appear to have inspired the persecution of Jews, nor did Jews constitute a group staunchly opposed to the Visgothic monarchy until the end of the seventh century. No Jewish revolts are known to have occurred before this time, when apparently a revolt, an authentic or supposed plot against King Egica, was to have taken place, thereby providing the monarch with the pretext for the drastic measure of attempting to turn Jews into slaves. If indeed it truly existed, such a plot could largely be explained with reference to the century of persecution Jews had suffered. Everything points to the fact that these discriminatory measures were inspired by religious zeal. Several doctrinal treatises written by Isidore of Seville (ca. 560–636), for example, are tantamount to diatribes against Judaism although Isidore objected to King Sisebut's attempts to convert Jews by force.[5] Isidore preferred persuasion as the best method of evangelizing but did not clearly come out against the violence of the period.

As at the end of the fifteen century with the forerunners of the creation of the Inquisition, in the Visigothic period some of the harshest critics of Jews were converts, former Jews who persecuted their former coreligionists. Such is the case of Julian of Toledo, a member of a family of converts, who wrote several harshly polemical works aimed at convincing Jews to renounce their false beliefs and embrace Catholicism. Finally, the Toledan councils, with several notable exceptions, produced a body of theoretical work that not only aimed at clarifying issues of dogma but also, when it did not directly inspire discriminatory measures taken by the civilian authorities, almost always supported them. Royal power and the Church collaborated closely to uproot Judaism, albeit for different reasons. The bishops were primarily concerned with Jewish proselytism and secondarily with the danger of contamination that converts represented—an issue that would reappear to justify the expulsion of 1492.[6] As for the Visigothic monarchy, from Recared on the clear intent was to stop a form of religious dissidence that carried visions of a very different political and religious future. Religious motivations and the determination to unify the kingdom joined to destroy peninsular Judaism, a clear antecedent to the situation at the beginning of modern times.

Jews in Muslim Spain

Under these conditions it is not at all strange that the Jewish community, overwhelmed by ill treatment, its identity and very existence both threatened, felt little sympathy for the Visigothic monarchy. Sánchez-Albornoz called Jews the "fifth column" at the time of the Muslim invasion in the eighth century, and later during the Middle Ages what was derogatively referred to as "ghetto treason" became one of the most well-established arguments concerning the "loss of Spain." This treason is not documented in the sources and probably only refers to some kind of vague hope of liberation from a power that was enslaving Jews. What is certain is that Jews welcomed the Islamic invaders with open arms. It is a matter of debate whether or not they surrendered Toledo to Tarik, although it seems likely that the Muslim general entrusted Jews with the defense of the city after its conquest, a procedure repeated in many other conquered cities.[7] In Córdoba, Jews took on attacking troops; in Seville (712), Muza, another Muslim general, left them to guard the city. The same occurred in Granada. Usually, "When the Moslems arrived in a city where there were Jews, they left them the responsibility of guarding the city along with other invaders, thus allowing them to continue their military campaign without diminishing their troops."[8]

Compliance of this sort argued for greater benevolence toward Jews on the part of the peninsula's new rulers. It is well to note, however, that there were other circumstances denoting a more favorable relationship, among them the lack of importance Muslims accorded to the conversion to Islam. Moreover, Muslims considered Christians and Jews as both sons of Abraham and monotheists, the same as themselves. As such, both deserved special treatment as defined in the *dhimma* (the "writ of protection" statute applicable to these two minorities). In practice, this resulted essentially in freedom of religion and the possibility of benefiting from a certain autonomy, for example, the power to name representatives who spoke on their behalf. In exchange, it is true, these minorities were subjected to a state of submission and dependency in relation to Islam. In short, Jews were tolerated in the same way as Christians. They were guaranteed personal security and the right to pursue their professional activities so long as their authority did not extend to Islamic believers. That was not always possible, however; there were occasionally serious conflicts between Muslims and Jews.

Despite these circumstances, it is probable that many Jews converted to Islam in the course of the eighth, ninth, and tenth centuries. Estimates show that by the end of the twelfth century 80 percent of the peninsular's Hispano-Roman population had done so. This group included part of the Jewish population although no exact sources or figures can be cited. Nevertheless, Jewish communities revived throughout the peninsula, and in some cases they assumed a high level of importance and activity. This did not occur in Córdoba, capital of al-Andalus, where some of the first emirs did not want the number of Jews to increase. On the other hand, sources in other cities attest to the rebirth and vitality of the Jewish communities. That was true, for example, in Granada and Tarragona, which Arabic sources sometimes cite as "Jewish cities," as well as in Jaén, Zaragoza, Seville, Almería, Barcelona, and, above all, Lucena, where the Moors lived in isolation on the outskirts of town. The Jewish historian Yitzbak Baer even cites the case of a deacon of German descent who moved to Zaragoza in the year 839 and embraced Judaism, married a Jewess, and wrote several works against Christianity that antagonized the Christians (known as *mozárabes*) living in Córdoba.[9]

Initially, the Jews living in Spain were not engrossed in any particular vocation; some were even involved in rural activities and agriculture. At a relatively early date, however, some Jews began to specialize in commerce and money-lending. They also established a near-monopoly over the slave trade, which arrived in Spain from Eastern Europe through a route via Verdun and the Rhone Valley. Jews also had control over the "fabrication" of eunuchs for harems, the particular specialty of those in the Andalusian town of Lucena. At the very least, Muslim rulers delegated these and other unpopular activities (including the collection of taxes) to Jews. This policy allowed Jews—or at least some of them—to achieve a measure of economic prosperity although it also exposed them, especially during periods of recession and crisis, to popular wrath inasmuch as they were seen to have both created and profited from the difficulties of the moment.

There were also those Jews who reached the heights of power thanks to the confidence of the caliphate's authorities or monarchs of the *taifa* [independent Muslim-ruled principality]. Very well known in this regard is Hasday ben-Saprut, who during the time of Abd-ar-Rahman III (912–961), served initially as court physician and translator of scientific works and later as a diplomat and overseer of international trade. Hasday figures as the prototypical public Jew, who while occupying important positions at the court played an essential role in the development of the Córdoba's Hebrew community owing to his efforts to transform the city into a prominent Jewish center.

There are also references to Jews who served as viziers in Zaragoza, Seville, and Almería. The most noted success is probably that of Samuel ha-Naguid, better known as Nagrella, who until his death in 1056 was the de facto ruler of Granada, directing both its internal politics and its diplomatic and military activities. Nagrella was also one of the greatest Hispano-Hebrew poets. It is, however, an exaggeration to portray him as an authentic military hero leading the troops of Granada.

It is nevertheless clear that some Jews were completely able to integrate themselves into political life in al-Andalus in spite of the dhimma's theoretical prohibition against Jews having authority over believers. In any event, the idea should not be overstated. Those individual Jews who had power constituted only a tiny minority, whereas the vast majority lived in much less brilliant conditions. Moreover, these heights of glory in the service of princes tended in many cases to be quite precarious. Jews who held positions of authority were likely to suffer disgrace and death whenever they lost their master's confidence. Finally, these prominent "court" Jews provoked strong popular hatred among Muslims who felt that the power conferred to such individuals made a mockery of the dhimma, a doctrine theoretically intended to keep them in a situation of humiliation and inferiority.

This brings us to the much-discussed question of the golden age of Judaism in Muslim Spain. The last years of the Caliphate of Córdoba and the era coinciding with the reigns of the taifas, which lasted until the middle of the twelfth century, represent the great era for the Hebrew community of al-Andalus.

Without renouncing either its faith or traditions, the Jewish elite assimilated the best of Islamic civilization and thus rose to an exceptional cultural level. They learned the Arabic language in which philosophical treatises were written while expressing themselves in Hebrew, sometimes in Aramaic in their poetry.

Hasday is known as the traditional forerunner of this cultural movement in the Jewish community of al-Andalus, which later flourished in the eleventh and twelfth centuries. In Zaragoza during the first half of the eleventh century there was a fertile nucleus of writers, poets, and philosophers whose main representative was Ibn Gabirol, known as Avicebrón in Christian universities. A philosopher inspired by neo-Platonism, and in turn one who inspired scholastic thinkers such as Duns Scotus, Gabirol became suspect in the eyes of his fellow Jews due to his pantheistic tendencies. During the twelfth century the great figure in Hebrew culture in al-Andalus was a Córdoban, Maimonides (1135–1204). Rabbi, physician, philosopher, and author of the *Guide for the Perplexed,* a confrontation between the Bible, Jewish thought, and Aristotelian philosophy, Maimonides attempted to prove that there was no contradiction between faith and reason. Thomas Aquinas, Albert the Great, and various other European Christian authors read his works and were inspired by them.

The example of Maimonides shows clearly the extraordinary development of intellectual life among Jews in al-Andalus up until the arrival of the Almohads. It is understandable that many authors have referred to this exceptional period as a "golden age." Baer, however, does not accept the expression: "Jewish culture was able to flourish only due to the negligence and religious and moral laxness of the governors and not as a consequence of a clearly defined politics of tolerance and individual freedom."[10] Baer is certainly correct. There are indeed Jews who retrospectively idealize the situation of their forefathers in al-Andalus. Some authors have even gone so far as to speak of medieval Spain's "three cultures." Nothing of the sort occurred. Medieval Spain knew only two dominant and dominating cultures: first Muslims, then Christians. Jews were incorporated into the first and then the second, but there was no separate Jewish culture as such, unless this term is used in the most restricted sense to identify the religious and spiritual norms as practiced in the *aljamas* (political and religious assemblies of Jews in synagogues).[11] Jews continued to be Jews in al-Andalus from the religious point of view; but in every other way, they adopted the dominant cultural models. In the first place, they adopted the Arabic language, thereby gaining access to an extraordinarily abundant literary, philosophical, and scientific capital. Their perfect assimilation with regard to Arabic culture was the ticket to their success and relative prestige in al-Andalus. Nonetheless, this intellectual prestige did not necessarily translate into an improvement in the living conditions of the majority of the Hebrew people. The very case of Maimonides demonstrates the point. Born in Córdoba, he studied Arabic until eighteen years of age. When the North Africans arrived, instead of moving to Christian Spain, as did many of his fellow Jews, he pretended to convert to Islam and left for Fez, then for Cairo, where he spent the rest of his days. There he returned to Judaism and wrote his entire philosophical corpus in Arabic, basing it on Arabic sources. Can Maimonides be considered a representative of Jewish culture in al-Andalus? No. In every way, he remains an eminent representative of Arabic culture, although he later returned to the Judaism of his youth.

It is therefore excessive to idealize this period and continue to speak of Jewish cultural splendor. It is also wrong to refer to this era as a time when Jews, Muslims and Christians lived side by side in mutual tolerance and respect. The Arabs were tolerant of the Jews because of their scarce numbers and out of necessity. Something similar occurred in Christian Spain. All in all, the situation changed radically with the arrival of the Almorávides and especially the Almohads, both Moorish tribes from North Africa. The strict legalistic sentiments of the Almorávids (1086–1143) contrasted sharply with the freedom of action and thought found in al-Andalus although it does not appear that any particularly harsh measures were enacted against Jews.

This was not the case with the Almohads (1156–1269). Their narrow and strict interpretation of Islamic law and conviction that they possessed the one and only truth meant that Jews either had to convert or suffer martyrdom. At this point the majority of Jews then moved to the northern Christian provinces, where they were welcomed with open arms by, for example, King Jaime I of Aragon. Jewish prosperity and cultural life in al-Andalus was over, never to return. Those who remained in Muslim territories after the fall of the Almohads constituted a minority about which little information exists. We can only assume that their lot had little in common with the one they previously enjoyed.

Jews in Christian Spain

Christian monarchs welcomed all Jews fleeing Almohadan persecution, helping them to settle in their territories and at the same time taking great advantage of their services. This constituted nothing out of the ordinary. The prodigious project of colonization and repopulation connected with the Reconquest required the collaboration of all vital forces.[12] The advances of the Reconquest posed serious economic, administrative, and diplomatic problems. Jews, or rather those belonging to the Jewish social elite, offered three distinct advantages in this respect. First of all, many specialized in commerce and craftsmanship and were in a good position to begin economic life in the still relatively undeveloped lands of Christian Spain. Second, some possessed property and wealth that enabled them to contribute to sovereigns' coffers and finance new conquests. Finally, Jews wrote and spoke Arabic, skills that allowed them to serve as intermediaries and essential helpers in contacts with the Muslim populations subject to the taifas monarchs. In addition, the Jews came to play their now-traditional role in economic life as tax collectors, administrators, and diplomats. We know that there was a Jew named Joseph ibn Salomon ibn Shoshan who advanced Alfonso VIII the money he needed to finance the expedition that would culminate in the great victory of Navas de Tolosa (1212). When Christians recovered the city of Seville, Alfonso X transformed the mosques into synagogues. Although contrary to canon law, this decision demonstrated the king's desire to compensate Jews for their assistance and their continuing willingness to contribute their support whenever possible.

We even have some evidence suggesting the direct, military participation of Jews in the battles of the Reconquest. In this regard Baer cites the division of properties made in Jerez de la Frontera in 1266 and refers to a document in which Jews were rewarded with certain lands and houses and are referred to as *ballesteros* (crossbow men or king's porters), which could mean they were soldiers. The others so rewarded were listed as officials of the king, that is, as regular collaborators of the crown. The document also suggests that their services in the conquest of that city were judged indispensable.[13]

In Aragon and Catalonia, similar situations evolved, some of which were even more significant than those in Castile. Jewish money contributed directly to finance the conquests of both Mallorca and Valencia. In return, the monarchs rewarded Jews with the right to collect many taxes and other state revenues. Thus, many bailiffs (*bailes*) and other subaltern officials of the royal administration were Jews. Such, for example, were the origins of the fortune and prestige that the De la Caballería family came to enjoy in Zaragoza.[14] As early as 1257 Don Yehudá ben Leví de la Caballería appears as the bailiff of Zaragoza. Three years later, the sovereign entrusted him with the collection of all state revenues in the Kingdom of Aragon. He was also bailiff of Valencia, where he owned lands and granaries.[15]

At the end of the thirteenth century Pedro III went even further in conferring Jews with high positions of power. The Ravaya brothers, for example, were authorized to sign, in the king's name, many directives relating to the distribution of arms and provisioning of, as well as other orders relating to, his vassals.[16] There is also the example of another Jew who was very influential in the court of Pedro III: Samuel ibn Manasseh. Educated in Arabic culture, Samuel served as the king's interpreter in negotiations with the Moorish kings of the peninsula and North Africa. To tell the truth, however, Samuel ibn

Manasseh, although formally a Jew, had very little to do with his coreligionists. He paid no tributes and never wore any distinguishing signs. Rather, he dressed and acted in every way like a Christian, riding a horse and using arms as any Aragonese noble.[17]

In general, it can be said that a large part of the royal patrimony was managed by Jews, all of which contravened canonical norms, as repeatedly reiterated by the Church. According to canon law, Jews were not to hold public offices that would result in their authority over Christians. Once in a while, kings were obliged to take a step backward and remove Jews from power, but they did not waste much time in turning to them again, less out of any particular sympathy for the Jewish community than because they considered the services of some Jews as indispensable. It was only at the end of the thirteenth century, in both Aragon and Castile, that Christians began to be entrusted with the tasks and social functions previously monopolized by Jews.

It is not easy to specify, even in an approximate manner, the demographic weight of the peninsular Jews. There are great variations and disparities among historians' estimates. For thirteenth-century Castile, Luis Suárez Fernández calculates a Jewish population of a hundred thousand.[18] Judging on the basis of a 1290 tax poll, Baer believes there were no more than 3,600 Jewish taxpayers in all the kingdoms and territories of Castile. Because these were taxpayers (*pecheros*), male heads of household, we can multiply by an average multiplier of 5 to obtain the number of corresponding inhabitants, an estimated twenty thousand Jews.[19] Julio Valdéon Baruque's figures are much higher for the fourteenth century: between 180,000 and 250,000 for the year 1370.

The truth is that no exact calculation of the Jewish population is possible. Suárez and especially Baer use figures that do not fit with what we know of later periods. Scrutinized carefully, they appear to be far too low. Valdéon's figures are more acceptable. It seems reasonable to assume that at the end of the fourteenth century the Jewish population of Castile was in the neighborhood of 250,000 individuals. If we subtract from this figure those Jews who converted to Christianity after the crisis of 1391, some two hundred thousand but probably fewer, and then add a growth factor due to the demographic recovery during the fifteenth century—from which Jews like Christians should have benefited—we are not far from 150,000. This is the usual figure given for the Jewish population of the Castilian territories at the eve of the expulsion of 1492.

The territorial distribution provides more concrete indications. During the thirteenth century, four cities stand out for the size of their Jewish communities: Burgos, in the north, Toledo, in the center, and Seville and Córdoba, in the south. Burgos was home to between 120 and 150 Jewish families, that is, fewer than a thousand individuals in all. Toledo and its surrounding area had one of the highest concentrations of Jews. According to the tax poll of 1290, some 350 families lived there, leading Luis Suárez Fernández to consider Toledo "a veritable metropolis of Castilian Judaism." The same tax poll indicates that Seville harbored around two hundred families and as many as twenty-three synagogues. Outside of these four cities, the Jewish population was much more dispersed, although, at least in the region between Burgos and Toledo, they tended to concentrate in communities of fifty to a hundred families. In Avila in 1303, Jews owned some forty houses in the neighborhood of the cathedral. The first mention of Jews in Valladolid figures in a document from 1167. In the following century, one gets the impression that this community achieved a certain level of prosperity with its own butcher and at least two synagogues. Guadalajara had at least thirty families. The Jews of Navarre enjoyed a privileged position for the period. They lived in prosperous aljamas in Tudela, Pamplona, Estella, Sangüesa, Viana, Los Arcos, Olite, and Peralta.

Figures are equally vague about the Jewish population in the Kingdom of Aragon. We only know that in Aragon at the beginning of the thirteenth century there were eleven Jewish communities, three main ones (Zaragoza, Huesca, and Calatayud) and eight secondary ones (Teruel, Daroca, Tarazona, Egea, Alagón, Jaca, Montclús, and Barbastro).[20] The Catalonian Jewish communities were probably the most numerous in the entire peninsula. Although they represented no more than 3 to 5 percent of the population, they formed a homogeneous group concentrated in a few cities, first of all, Barcelona, then Vilafranca del Penedés, Tarragona, Montblanc, Lérida, Balaguer, Tárrega, Gerona, and Besalú. By the end of the thirteenth century the Kingdom of Valencia purportedly had as many as 250 Jewish families established in Valencia, Játiva, Castellón, Denia, and Murviedro. As for Mallorca, Baer is of the opinion that its Jewish community was the most commercially dynamic in medieval Europe. Many of its members were navigators and cartographers who, thanks to their theoretical and practical expertise in nautical science, played an important role in the voyages of exploration and discovery in the Atlantic. Mallorcan Jews also had commercial interests throughout the Mediterranean, especially in North Africa where they had friends and relatives. Nevertheless, it does not seem that they enjoyed the same prosperity as Christian merchants.[21]

Jews commonly called their neighborhoods *kahal,* a term etymologically related to the Catalonian word *call,* itself a Latin version of the original Hebrew that we will later find in the Spanish word *calle* (street). These linkages lead Luis Suárez Fernández to contemplate an early and close connection between urban life and Judaism.[22] Several important Jewish settlements were indeed located in city centers: in Barcelona near the cathedral, in Burgos near the castle, and in

Toledo not far from the city center. Baer suggests, on the contrary, that before being confined in urban ghettos during the fourteenth-century persecutions Jews preferred to settle in small towns and villages, the latter above all inasmuch as villages were thought to offer greater economic and political security. Moreover, Hebrew moral literature recommended villages over cities.[23]

This problem is closely related to the activities in which Jews exercised in Spanish society. The common medieval topos that can even be found in the anti-Semitic diatribes of Andrés Bernáldez, priest at Los Palacios, during the end of the fifteenth century, is that of the Jew a city-dweller, practicing occupations that correspond to this preferably urban setting: financial affairs, commerce, craftsmanship, and liberal or intellectual professions, thus excluding all agricultural work.[24]

In reality, that stereotype does not hold up. In the first centuries of the Middle Ages Jews practiced nearly the same array of labor activities as Christians. The specialization in determined roles of clear social significance was the lot of a small minority that due to its wealth, prestige, and influence attracted the attention of the Christian masses. Yet the existence of such a minority should in no way obfuscate the fact that most Jews lived in much more modest conditions, similar in most ways to their Christian neighbors. Béatrice Leroy has reconstructed the history of a Jewish family from Tudela until its exile to Cairo, after the expulsion of 1492. Its first documented members, in 1167, were vineyard owners and wheat farmers.[25] Indeed, until at least the thirteenth century Jews were mainly farmers and cattle-raisers and lived in the countryside and in villages. Baer affirms that the increase in Jewish settlements in the backward villages of Andalusia as early as the beginning of the fourteenth century can only be explained by the existence of a relatively significant Jewish farming population.[26]

In tenth-century Catàlonia several documents attest to Jews buying and selling land, farming, and harvesting the vines and fields themselves. In the twelfth century, the *Fueros generales* (General Statute Laws) of Aragon and Navarre mention Jews living on royal estates and paying the king taxes on produce from their fields and vineyards.[27] Nonetheless, to own land does not necessarily meant that one farms it personally. Even though it is possible that farming was only a secondary activity for most Jews, their rural presence among farmers and cattle-raisers cannot be completely denied, at least until the thirteenth century. In fact, the laws of 1282 and 1293 prohibited Jews from owning farm property. They also required Jews to sell the land they owned within a year, a requirement implying Jewish ownership of such property before that date. Christian society subsequently proceeded to separate Jews from farming and cattle-raising activities. Later measures, almost unenforceable in.

practice, attempted to prevent Jews from exercising trades and entering small businesses, especially if they worked for Christians.

The objective of these laws was to avoid all contact between Christians and Jews and ensure that Christians not depend upon Jews for certain trades and vice versa. This is the interpretation offered by J. M. Monsalvo Antón, and I believe it to be correct.[28] I would only add the following observation: Was there not also some fear of Jewish competition? We have indirect evidence of this hypothesis because there were also relatively experienced Christian artisans at the time, a fact that invalidates Américo Castro's thesis about the incapacity of the Christian caste to work as craftsmen and the necessity of seeking out Moors and Jews to "have things made." In Germany, something similar had taken place when as a result of various measures despoiling Jews of their wealth and subsequent mistreatment and persecution they were pushed into becoming money lenders. Baer thinks that this was also true of Spain from the thirteenth century on. Similar factors were at work in reducing the economic personality of Jews to something closer to the social status of the German Jew.

In the cities, whether large or small, many Jews had shops or artisanal workshops to practice their trade or craft but in the same proportions, or sometimes lesser proportions, than Christians. The theme of usury that would resonate loudly throughout the fourteenth-century crisis does not seem to have been that relevant before this period. It was only in the thirteenth century that it became illegal for Christians in Spain to collect interest on debts from other Christians. The same prohibition existed between Jews but not between persons of different religions. Some Jews took advantage of laws enabling them to enter into economic activities despite difficulties due to money shortages. Alfonso X's legal code constituting the laws of Castile, the *Siete Partidas,* had fixed the interest rate at a three-to-four ratio. If three were lent, four, or 33.3 percent, were owed, a rate that remained unchanged until the end of the Middle Ages. In Aragon, the Courts of Gerona (1241) fixed a much lower rate, 20 percent. In most cases it was applied to selling commonly used items (such as cloth) on credit. In 1264 a Jew from Tudela gave the rich the following piece of advice: "Choose to be a worker or a merchant; because if you can lend your money at interest, take advantage of the opportunity, don't miss it."[29]

In any case it is excessive and unjust to attribute to all peninsular Jews what was in fact a characteristic of only a small minority of them. The same is true of high-level peninsular and international business affairs and financial matters. Tax collection was in the hands of a few rich Jews, but the Christian population tended to identify all Jews with that small minority. It is well to note that over time, as an established Christian bourgeoisie was in the process of forming, it was also beginning to replace Jews in roles they had occupied in economic life. Christians were not, due to their religion, unable to exercise economic tasks that in no way were a Jewish monopoly.

From a legal standpoint Jews in Spain constituted a separate community alongside two others, Christian and Muslim. Luis Suárez Fernández writes that Jewish society was a microsociety parallel to Christian society. The term is appropriate and takes into account historical reality. Jews did form a microsociety, with its strong points and its defects, but which, on the whole, remained relatively autonomous. In my opinion this autonomy caused the disappearance of Spanish Judaism in 1492. These three communities were not at all on an equal plane. Christian culture was by far the dominant one in all areas, whereas the two others were always tolerated as minorities. This tolerance implies Jewish and Muslim inferiority with respect to Christians, a status justifying the fact that Jews and Muslims paid much higher taxes. In Castile during the twelfth century, in addition to the poll tax Jews as well as Christians paid the crown the *tercia* tax on revenues and other taxes. These included ordinary and extraordinary services, the duty to pay, like Christians, fees to municipalities, taxes to use public services and pastures, plus road tolls and cattle tolls. In addition, money was owed to the Church, including tithes, first fruits, and other taxes. In Navarre, the Jews' contribution or tribute (the *pecha*) was calculated according to the size of the population in each synagogue assembly. According to the tax list of 1294, Jews alone paid 22 percent of all direct taxes in the Kingdom of Aragon, and that figure does not include temporary exactions, forced loans, and other contributions.[30]

As clearly stated in the *Fuero de Teruel* (1176), in Christian Spain the status of Jews was that of royal serfs. As a property owned by the king, administratively, Jews belonged to the Royal Treasury. For that reason, if ever a Jew was physically harmed or murdered it was the Royal Treasury, not the family of the victim, that received indemnities because it was understood that the kingdom had suffered a loss.

In mid-thirteenth-century Castile, Alfonso X devised regulations concerning the legal situation of Jews. The *Partidas* authorized the presence of Jews in the society "because they live as if forever in captivity and as a remembrance of those men from their lineage who crucified our Lord Jesus Christ." After this preamble setting the limits of tolerance in strict and injurious terms, indicating Jews as deicidal (Christ-murderers) according to consistent Church doctrine, the document continues to define the legal status of Jews. Whereas the practice of the Jewish religion was permitted, all proselytizing remained forbidden under penalty of death. The same penalty applied to any Christian or Muslim who converted to Judaism. Existing synagogues could be restored or repaired, but no new constructions were allowed. Despite the recommendations made by Pope Innocent IV, the rights to possess and read books of Jewish law, observe the Sabbath, and celebrate other Jewish holidays were rescinded. Jews and Christians were nevertheless granted equal rights in legal matters before the courts.[31] Later a series of discriminatory measures were enacted against Jews that included a ban on holding public office or entering certain professions, medicine among them. The ban extended to sharing meals with Christians, caring for Christian children, and entrusting Jewish children to Christians as well as a ban on sexual relations with Christians. Finally, there was the obligation of wearing on one's person a visible distinctive sign of the Jewish faith.

Many of these bans and obligations were merely theoretical, such as the prohibition against exercising the medical profession and the obligation to wear distinctive signs. In everyday life Jews did not distinguish themselves from their fellow inhabitants by their clothes except in Catalonia, where Jews apparently wore the *capa redonda,* a large, round, hooded cape similar to that worn by friars and priests. Catalonian Jews were supposed to sew a special sign into their clothes according to Jaime III's laws, but the sign could easily be hidden.[32]

As a result of strong fiscal pressures Jews formed a separate entity and, as such, enjoyed a certain type of autonomy, albeit one that depended directly on the monarch. This autonomous entity, an aljama, was not to be understood in a territorial sense. The aljama is neither a ghetto nor a neighborhood separate from the rest of the population in which Jews had to live. In fact, it was only at the end of the Middle Ages that Jews would be enclosed in separate neighborhoods. At least until the end of the thirteenth century Spanish Jews enjoyed the freedom to live wherever they chose, although in practice they usually preferred to cluster together on certain streets. The aljama was thus a corporate community, a political-religious body ruled by its own juridical standards. In Castile at a relatively early date, various aljamas named legal representatives who occasionally gathered into an assembly to examine cases and determine which issues were of interest to the entire Jewish community of the kingdom. For Jews, this assembly came to resemble the parliament, the popular assembly of Castile. The situation, however, was different in both Navarre and in the Kingdom of Aragon, where each aljama had complete autonomy. In Castile, the king named, for the entire kingdom, a *rab* (major judge) who directed the entire Jewish community and served as an intermediary between it and the crown. But the existence of this official rab was a later phenomenon and only became common practice in other areas in the fifteenth century. The institution held not only undeniable advantages but also disadvantages for Jews. Convinced that the king was their main defender and they depended directly on him, Jewish representatives closely collaborated with royal power and helped it grow strong. At times of political crisis, however, that attitude made Jews a target for opposing parties.

At the local level, the aljama formed an autonomous legal and administrative entity. It had its own magistrates, rabbis, judges, and tax collectors for special taxes on domestic animals, wine, weddings, burials meant to offset community expenses such as rabbinical schools, places of worship, and assistance to the poor and infirm. The aljama enacted statutes or ordinances (*taccanot*), often written in Hebrew and Castilian, for its internal government. It functioned in much the same manner as the Christians' municipal councils.

We see the same evolution over time within aljamas and in councils. Initially, the officials running them were primarily senior citizens (*mucaddemim*) who were reelected each year in free elections. Only in the event of disagreement did the major rab interfere to appoint officials, judges, overseers, treasurers, and inspectors for public matters. Later these roles devolved into hereditary offices held by a few privileged families who came to monopolize the management of aljamas. The aljama of Barcelona, head of an extensive district that in 1332 included Vilafranca del Penedés, Cervera, Manresa, and Caldes de Montbui, was reorganized in 1327 to emulate a Christian municipal council. Its Council of Thirty resembled Barcelona's Council of One Hundred. Furthermore, the aljama regulated everything concerning the religious, social, legal, and economic life of its members. Three features of that role can be distinguished: tax collection, administration of justice, and organization of religious and cultural life.

The aljama was responsible for collecting contributions owed to the crown, whether ordinary or extraordinary, and sharing the tax burden among its members. Occasionally, this produced some tense moments. Like Christian councils, aljamas included individuals from all socioeconomic levels. On one hand, there were the very rich financiers and merchants who had direct dealings with the court, as did other nobles and prelates; on the other, there were virtual paupers and indigents; in between these two extremes was a middle class of retailers, artisans, and farmers. Thus, confrontations between the wealthy and the poor often arose during the division and collection of contributions. The powerful established minority was often able to exempt itself from paying its fair share, one that corresponded to its fortune, and sometimes even obtained additional privileges from the king, as did the Christian hidalgos. In such cases, as in Christian society, the burden fell on the rest of the mass of taxpayers. A natural aversion between this majority and the privileged minority was provoked. Thus, in Zaragoza in 1294 a rebellion emerged against the privileges of the "great taxpayers," the powerful minority, and the way they divided taxes, which allowed the wealthy to unjustly benefit from the process.[33]

In addition, the aljama had penal jurisdiction over its members. In litigation between Christians and Jews, a mixed tribunal had to be formed with representatives from each religion. Jewish complaints had to be resolved according to Jewish law, the Torah. Neglecting to respect the Sabbath or any other infringement of the religious norms prescribed by the Torah constituted a crime punishable by serious sanctions. The execution of sentences, however, was entrusted to the king's officials, who consistently respected the decisions of the alajma's judges. Crimes committed against the existence of the Jewish community by the so-called *malsines* (turncoats or backbiters) constituted one particular set of cases. Anything that could damage the reputation of the aljama was considered to be a very serious matter, especially such infringements as false accusations, defamation, denunciations [against the Jewish community], or entertaining Gentiles by recounting foolish stories about the law and Jewish religion. In such instances the aljama had a terrible weapon, the *herem*, a kind of excommunication from the Jewish world.

Judges were also able to hand down decisions against the accused and order severe punishments ranging from mutilations to amputations and even the death sentence. Baer describes the case of a Jewish youth from an illustrious family but accused of backbiting by his coreligionists in Barcelona around the year 1280. King Pedro III turned the case over to the rabbis and ordered that their sentence be executed. The youth was left to bleed to death publicly in front of the Jewish cemetery.[34] In Seville in 1312 the aljama asked the king's permission to judge a certain Jew who had taken to denouncing his fellow Jews individually and the community as a whole. Their request was accepted, and the man was condemned to the gallows.[35] The last death sentence pronounced against malsines in Castile seems to have been carried out in 1377 against Yosef Pichó. In 1380, Juan I, apparently shocked by this event, had the Courts of Soria abolish the aljamas' privilege of pronouncing death sentences, thereby leaving Jews without the ultimate means of defending themselves against coreligionists.

As for cultural and religious life in Spain's aljamas, it was dramatically altered between the twelfth and thirteenth centuries by two parallel currents: on one hand, the advent of controversies surrounding Maimonides' philosophy, and on the other the movement toward a purer and more orthodox form of Jewish religious practice.

Maimonides' *Guide to the Perplexed*, written in Arabic in 1190, was translated into Hebrew and came to Spain in that form via Catalonia. This relatively rapid transmission shows the intermediary role played by Catalonian aljamas that bridged peninsular and European Judaism.[36] Throughout the Middle Ages there was never interruption in the contact between the various strains of the Jewish Diaspora. In the second half of the twelfth century Benjamin de Tudela analyzed all the European countries and some Asian countries where Jewish communities existed in order to examine the various tendencies and spiritual currents in Judaism. The great debate revolved around the issue of how to interpret the doctrinal books of the Hebrew tradition. Should they be read in the strict literal sense, or was it possible to consider at least parts of them as metaphorical or allegorical? Beyond this controversy, a work such as that by Maimonides interpreted other aspects of the doctrine in terms of Aristotle, who had been introduced in Spain around this date thanks to the work of peninsular Arab philosophers. Philosophical ideas commonly referred to as Averroist were widely known in Christian theology at the time, and these led to intense polemics whose great synthesis was achieved in the work of Thomas Aquinas.[37]

Maimonides' contribution was to attempt to reconcile philosophical rationalism and the Jewish faith. For the most part that was achieved by going beyond the apparently archaic and irrational aspects of religion to show that, on the whole, faith did not contradict philosophy. The Averroist currents undoubtedly carried within them the germs of rationalism. In the best cases they limited themselves to defending a merely allegorical interpretation of the Scriptures and reducing precepts to their symbolic value.

From this point the theory of double truth was but a step away. Some made that step and concluded that one truth would be valid for the masses and require consistent dogma and precepts and the other would be acceptable to the elite, who outwardly pretended to share the faith of the humble but were in fact unable to believe in what they judged as foolishness. These Averroist tendencies gave rise to a kind of religious indifference or lack of enthusiasm for religion that went as far as actual unbelief and materialism. This phenomenon has been sufficiently documented for "court" Jews and for those in the liberal professions (physicians, for example) who were accustomed to associating with Christians of the same cultural background. In short, these people considered themselves superior to the popular masses, which included other Jews. Some court Jews demonstrated great skepticism with regard to doctrine and did not bother to respect the norms imposed on Christians and Jews. They did not take Jewish laws seriously and neglected their religious obligations; they kept Christian concubines, slept with prostitutes, and played dice, for example. In essence, they lived a decadent Sybaritic life without moral or religious scruples.[38] Baer reiterates that the descendants of these courtesans were the first to deny their faith and commit treason against their people in the great upheaval during the years between 1391 and 1415. The grandsons of these apostates—converts from then on—would be accused before the

Inquisition's tribunals as unbelievers for whom man had been created to be born and die, like plants and animals, without a spiritual perspective.[39]

Some rabbis gave an enthusiastic reception to Maimonides' ideas, which seemed more in line with the vital and intellectual needs of the period. Others, instead, were appalled by what they considered to be a dangerous doctrinal deviation likely to lead to the disappearance of the traditional aspects of the Jewish religion, and therefore they stuck to the letter of the ancient scriptures and the laws contained within them. Believing that prematurely reading certain authors could mitigate the faith of the young and untutored, a Catalonian rabbi, Rashba, better known as Adret, prohibited the study of metaphysics, Greek philosophy (specifically Aristotle's works), and natural science. The ban was to apply to all under the age of twenty-five and all works on these subjects, whether in Arabic or in translation. The prohibition, however, did not include astronomy and medicine nor the works of Maimonides himself. Baer is of the opinion that Adret's anathema (1305) had a limited impact on some Jewish intellectuals who were very attracted by new currents of thought. Moreover, Adret insisted on strictly observing religious law, following the sacred texts to the letter, and the necessity of prayer and fervent religious practice. Adret believed that this was the only way to placate the wrath of God in order to avoid the persecutions and misfortunes of the Jewish people, which he interpreted as punishment for their sins. Abiding by Jewish law had to come before everything else, including any order dictated by Christian authorities. Adret thereby attempted to give new vigor to Judaism, inviting it to be more forceful, less ashamed of itself, and prepared to assume the mission of reclaiming the wholeness of its religious belief system.

Adret's attitude reinforced the resurgent religious zeal developing in the aljamas. Many Jews were indeed scandalized by the attitudes of court Jews who used their interpretation of Maimonides as a justification for their own misconduct. In reaction to this attitude there were also mystical and pietistic currents that, to a certain degree, can be compared to what the mendicant orders of Dominicans and Franciscans were practicing in Christian society at the time. In other words there was a similar return to more orthodox and traditional forms of piety, which entailed observing all aspects of religious law and accepting no compromise with the heathen concept of life or with philosophical rationalism.

Even the Jews' troubling material difficulties were interpreted as a sign from God—the price the chosen people gone astray had to pay. The mystical movement known as the cabala is the major exponent of this current. That typically Jewish gnostic movement attempted to adapt Aristotle's theory of the eternity of the world to the biblical dogma of creation. To do so, the cabala interposes a significant number of intermediaries between God and man. There are also mystical commentaries on the Torah in the cabala that rely on a variety of source materials: astronomy, cosmologny, physics, psychology, demonology, numerical symbolism, enigmas, and puns. The doctrine resulted in pure mysticism and fundamentalism: Jewish people, in spite of and due to their suffering, bore the origin of truth within their lineage. Any form of treason, compromise with Gentiles or philosophical rationalism, or activity in the service of Christians in the court, for example, or any sexual contact with a Christian, were considered criminal acts.[40] A Jew so engaged became a traitor to his people and delivered himself into the hands of Satan.

At the end of the thirteenth century widespread Messianism triumphed in this moral climate. Rabbis and "prophets" from Avila and Ayllon announced the coming of the Messiah for the year 5055/1295, which was to be preceded by a series of extraordinary phenomena and the blowing of a great horn. Many Jews prepared for this event that would bring them out of exile, fasting and distributing alms. On the appointed day they entered their synagogues dressed in white sheets, according to custom, but things did not turn out as they expected. The story goes that they saw colored crosses on the sheets instead of the Messiah, and some were disillusioned and became Christians.

This was the nature of life in the aljamas in Christian Spain during the twelfth and thirteenth centuries before the great crisis and persecutions that took place in the late Middle Ages. This era, approximately between the years 1148 and 1348, has remained in the collective memory of the Jewish people as a kind of golden age, one that can only be compared to the period they experienced in Muslim Spain before the arrival of the Almohades. Due to their numbers, the degree of autonomy they enjoyed, and their social role and position as intermediaries between Christian and Muslim cultures Jews provided a bridge between the East and the West, not only from economic, political, and diplomatic viewpoints but in cultural and philosophical matters as well. This was especially true of the splendor of Jewish Toledo at the time.

In many ways Toledo was like a new Jerusalem for Jews in that it had a simultaneously religious, philosophical, and economic focus of activity. Some of the relics of this culture are still preserved, such as the great synagogues of Santa María la Blanca del Tránsito and the so-called Casa del Greco, which is in reality Samuel ha-Levi's palace. They give an idea of the economic force and artistic refinement of Toledo's Jews in the twelfth and thirteenth centuries, especially in terms of their capacity to assimilate the most valuable contributions of two worlds in an admirable and original synthesis. Members of the Spanish Jewish elite were educated and adept in Arabic culture, which in the first centuries of the Middle Ages was much more brilliant than that of the Christian world.

Given their knowledge of the Arabic language, Jews were in direct contact with all the Islamic cultural areas from the Indian Ocean to the Atlantic, with its great centers of civilization—notably, Byzantium, Damascus, Cairo, and Baghdad. By as early as the eighth century the Eastern Arab world had compiled the scientific and philosophical legacy of Ancient Greece that was deposited in the great libraries of Alexandria, Antioch, and Carthage. Many works of physics, mathematics (Euclid, for example), and medicine (Hippocrates and Galen) were translated into Arabic. This cultural heritage was increased even further by what the Arabs learned from the best of Persian, Indian, and Chinese science. The cultural center of Córdoba alone boasted a prestigious library containing four hundred thousand volumes and two hundred thousand Greek, Latin, and Arabic manuscripts.

It was this scientific and philosophical abundance that made its way into the Western world in the beginning of the twelfth century through what has been somewhat abusively called Toledo's School of Translators. Although Toledo was rapidly transformed into the most important and prestigious center, Zaragoza and other cities between the Ebro and the Tajo Rivers were also much involved in the process. Jews played the prominent role in the transmission of knowledge because it was first a matter of translating Arabic texts into Spanish and then into Latin. Their knowledge of the Arabic language and culture made them key actors in this massive effort that culminated during the reign of Alfonso X el Sabio (the Sage) (1252–84).

It is not possible to analyze herein the overall Jewish contribution in as detailed manner as it deserves. I will limit myself to mentioning, as a case in point, that of a single individual, Abraham ibn Ezra. A Jew from Tudela, Ibn Ezra was an accomplished mathematician and an astronomer whose works, written in Hebrew, were quickly translated into romance languages, especially into Catalan.[41] Through this type of activity Spanish Jewish intellectuals during the twelfth and thirteenth centuries gained great prestige. Whereas this prestige was coveted by their Christian colleagues it also led to creating a positive image of Jews that continues to a certain extent into the modern age, as people traditionally well versed in the arts and sciences. In addition to the prestige and pride Spanish Jews felt for belonging to a kind of collective nobility, descendants claimed to belong to the tribe of Judah (not Jacob) and originate from the city of Jerusalem.

Undoubtedly, the situation of the Jews in Spain was much more favorable than in the rest of the European countries at the time. It is, however, important to attenuate the sometimes exaggerated idea of Spain's openness, respect, and tolerance for Jewish religion and culture. The reality was very different. There was never truly peaceful cohabitation or mutual respect for the dissident religious group. Like the *mudéjares* (Muslim subjects of Christian sovereigns), Jews were tolerated, which meant they were allowed to live and practice their religion because they were considered indispensable actors in economic life.[42]

The vicissitudes of the Reconquest of Spain obliged monarchs to rely on the services of all members of society, Christians and non-Christians alike. This was the nature of medieval tolerance, a more or less forced, as opposed to authentic, *convivencia.* One has to discard the idea of Spain as a model multireligious society in which the three religions or three cultures would have coexisted in mutual respect during the twelfth and thirteenth centuries on a privileged and ideal island in an ocean of intolerance and fanaticism. The three religions, Muslim, Christian, and Jewish, were never comparable in terms of dignity or status. Inasmuch as Muslims, like Christians, claimed to possess the revealed (one and only) truth, a truth exclusive of others, no mutual respect was possible between them. As for peninsular Judaism, both Muslims and Christians felt an identical contempt for it.

The presence of ecumenical projects at given points in time should not mislead us. In the *Libro del gentil y de los tres sabios* by Ramón Llull (d. 1315) an intellectual exchange among believers of the three religions is presented in order to try to discover which should be considered the most truthful. That is well and fine, but we must realize that such a debate was nothing but literary entertainment. The same author spent a good part of his life's work attempting to convert infidels. Llull requested permission from Jaime II to preach before Jews, not to exchange ideas with them but rather to convince them that they had to renounce their false beliefs. We can only suppose that his sermons were less ecumenical than his literary works. As for Alfonso X, sometimes presented as a paragon of tolerance for the support he gave to the translation work from Arabic, it is enough to examine his body of laws, the *Partidas,* to see where his true sentiments lay. He justified authorizing the presence of Jews in Spain "so that they could live as in permanent captivity and be remembered as the men whose forefathers crucified our Lord Jesus Christ." The same Alfonso X treated the Jewish and Muslim minorities in his territories quite harshly, especially toward the end of his reign when he began to impose a practice of politically isolating Moors and Jews and gradually reduced some of their previously obtained legal rights. In short, intellectual fraternization did not reach society at large.

Even more inexact than the subject of the three religions is that of the three cultures. In medieval Spain there were never more than two dominant cultures, Muslim and Christian, and one succeeded the other. Jews participated in both according to the region in which they lived. Jewish culture and the culture of the Jews should not be confused. In our time, Karl Marx, Freud, Einstein, and any others we can cite represent German culture more than Jewish culture just as Marcel Proust belongs more specifically to the French. That does not prevent us from detecting certain roots in these scientists, writers, or artists that could be attached to their Jewish religion of origin. Things were not so simple during the Middle Ages. Jews were very much immersed in the world of the aljamas in a way that has no equivalent in modern secular societies.

All in all, it is still not possible to speak of a strictly Jewish culture in an absolute sense. Jews adopted the language and culture of the society in which they lived: first the Muslim and then the Christian. Something similar occurred in golden age Spanish literature. Saint Teresa and Friar Luis de León are great Castilian writers who do not represent Jewish culture but rather partake in a cultural environment that already had nothing to do with Judaism. It seems inappropriate to speak in general terms of Spain's three cultures. This observation is aimed at all those theses and traditional histories that attempt to present medieval Spain as a blessed land for the free development of beliefs and ideas in stark contrast to the rest of the Eastern and Western world engulfed in fanaticism and intolerance.

It is worth clarifying this point. In Spain there were circumstances—the necessity of repopulating the land and cultivating and administrating land reconquered from the Moors—that impeded sovereigns from strictly observing the Roman Catholic Church's repeated recommendations. The Fourth Lateran Council (1215) reiterated that cohabitation between Christians and Jews constituted a grave danger for the former and thus should be reduced to a minimum (for example, to economic transactions). Otherwise, it advocated strict separation between the religions; Christians should not have Jewish servants, wet nurses, or doctors. By the same token, mixed marriages were forbidden and Jews were required to live in separate neighborhoods and wear distinctive signs to mark their Judaism. In no case were Jews to be given public responsibilities implying their authority over Christians. Jews were allowed to practice their religion, but with a high level of discretion given that the construction of new synagogues was banned. The objective of these recommendations was to end the "perfidy" of Jews who insisted upon negating the obvious truth that Jesus Christ was the announced Messiah. One of the principal roles assigned to the mendicant orders was precisely to preach to convince and convert Jews.[43]

Due to the particular set of conditions in Spain, monarchs could not apply all these Church recommendations in a consistent manner yet there is much evidence to show that the reigning mentality was the same as in the rest of Europe. In the Kingdom of Castile there is the example of the Synod of Zámora (1312). Here, with the participation of the bishops of the metropolitan province of Santiago, it was agreed to require the monarch to immediately apply anti-Jewish directives issued by the councils and the popes. These specifically included wearing a distinctive sign, prohibiting Jews to use Christian names, and banning them from holding offices that would imply their jurisdiction over Christians.[44] Moreover, Jews were forbidden to work in public on Sundays and Christian holidays or show themselves in public during Holy Week from Wednesday until Saturday. On Good Friday Jews were required to close their doors and windows "so as not to make a mockery of the Christians' remembrance of the Passion of Jesus Christ." In 1322 the papal legate presiding in Valladolid held a council and adopted various measures along the same lines. Jews were no longer allowed to enter churches, and Christians were no longer allowed to attend Jewish or Muslim weddings or funerals. Christians were also discouraged from having Jewish doctors or shopping in Jewish-owned stores. This is when the theme of the deicidal (Christ-murdering) people was reiterated; the faithful were called upon to reject *pro perfidis judaeis.*[45]

Numerous campaigns of proselytizing and literary polemics were aimed at demonstrating the falsehood of Judaism and the obstinacy of Jews. Arnaldo de Vilanova composed a treatise on the Trinity in which he referred to a celebrated text, *Pugio fidei adversus mauros et iudaeos,* written by a Catalonian Dominican, Ramón Marti. To best combat the Jews, the authors made great intellectual efforts. Some even learned Hebrew in order to refute the sources and demonstrate that rabbis were mistaken in their interpretations and were in fact deceiving their coreligionists. That is how Christians' Bible study programs originated and developed over the sixteenth century. A polemic was brewing involving Hebraicists (Friar Luis de León, for example) accused of preferring *hebraica veritas,* that is, the original text of the Bible, to the Church's traditional reading. In Murcia in 1263 there was a school of this type. For the most part these institutions had no scientific interests or intellectual curiosity; their role was to train missionaries to combat rabbis on their on ground and prepare for controversy.[46] Thus, the treatise written by Nicolás de Lira, *Postilla litteralis super Bibliam,* demonstrates the author's profound knowledge of Hebrew. De Lira condemned the Jews' error of not accepting Christ as the Messiah and explained the Bible's frequent references to the Trinity and the double nature (both human and divine) of the Son. Some Christian theologians, authors of anti-Jewish treatises, were converts who, as in other periods of history, were among the harshest critics in refuting their former coreligionists. Indeed, there were many conversions during these years although nothing like the number during the fifteenth century. One of the most famous was that of the Rabbi of Burgos, a doctor named Abner, baptized in 1320. He moved to Valladolid, where he became sacristan in a college called Alfonso de Valladolid. From then on attacks against Jews and Judaism were continuous. "Throughout the entire Middle Ages," writes Baer, "there was no Christian theologian who raged against the Talmud in as narrow and harsh a manner as did this Jewish apostate." To convert Jews the former rabbi did not back down from the use of force.

In the Kingdom of Aragon in the middle of the thirteenth century, mendicant orders initiated campaigns to convert Jews and Muslims. Dominicans were authorized to preach in synagogues, and Jews were obliged to listen to their sermons. A celebrated dispute in Barcelona in 1263 in the presence of Jaime I and Raymond of Penyafort (Raimundo de Peñaforte) opposed a Dominican converted from Judaism and a doctor and rabbi, Moses ben Namán (Nahmanides). The main intent was to demonstrate the Jews' error and obstinacy in continuing to wait for the Messiah.

In this decidedly anti-Jewish context there is no way to distance Spain from the rest of Europe. Rumors and accusations regarding the evil of the Hebrew people were abundant. Jews were accused of the ritual assassinations of Christian children and the profanation of the Host.[47] Added to these accusations, which were commonplace in Christian Europe, there were some typically Spanish issues such as the Jews' role in turning over the city of Toledo to the Moors in 711.

All of the above are unequivocal signs of a mentality that was anything but tolerant. For a time the political and economic state of affairs did not allow things to move to the breaking point. That, however, was to change over the following century, and the crisis period inaugurated would dramatically alter the Jews' situation ever after.

2

The Crisis in the Fourteenth Century

Contrary to Américo Castro's contention, I do not believe that the originality of medieval Spain can be attributed to the presence of religiously determined castes—Christians, Muslims, and Jews—as opposed to the rest of Europe during the same era where social differentiation relied on other bases such as the power of feudal lords and economic influence. It is difficult to follow the great Hispanic scholar when he affirms that caste determined social status in Spain. Jews were entrusted with intellectual and economic functions and Moors with trades, craftsmanship, and agricultural work, whereas power and prestige were reserved for Christians. In fact, many Christians worked in agriculture and commerce, and not all Jews were physicians, university scholars, and businessmen.

According to this premise, the transformations that occurred in the middle of the fourteenth century were not solely or mainly due to the Christians' desire to eliminate or destroy the other two castes through humiliation and persecution. Rather, it was due to a much more concrete and well-known matter: the economic, political, and social upheavals of the last two centuries of the Middle Ages, beginning with high mortality rates due to the massacres and epidemics sweeping Europe. The cultural zenith symbolized by Alfonso X's reign coincided with a phase of demographic and economic expansion.

It was the crisis in the fourteenth century that sharpened tensions and inaugurated an era of serious conflicts not only with regard to religion but also in every other arena. Loss of life was tremendous. Hundreds of thousands died, and an entire economic structure was demolished; ancient hierarchies partially disappeared, and some groups took advantage of the situation by seizing positions of power. Political life was thus affected by the consequences of this tremendously destabilizing, confusing experience. Factions fought for power, and, ultimately, Enrique de Trastámara [who became King Enrique II] defeated his brother, Pedro el Cruel [King Pedro I]. To win followers Enrique did not hesitate to offer pensions, domains, and privileges to newcomers who began to form a new kind of nobility—the so-called *mercedes enriqueñas* (untitled rich).

From this perspective it is necessary to focus on events that inaugurated a new course in the history of Spain. Little changed for *mudéjares* (Muslim subjects of Christian lords) subjected to a feudal type of exploitation; they continued to constitute cheap manual labor for secular and ecclesiastical lords. Instead, those most negatively affected by the changes were Jews who had gradually established themselves in high positions or become specialized in financial matters as tax collectors or lenders. During the crisis the popular masses' age-old hatred and resentment were directed against those Jews who were seen as the instruments and beneficiaries of their difficulties.

Rather than transformations in doctrine, the period of conflict was spurred by changes in existing social reality, and those changes tragically affected the condition of Jews not only in Spain but also in the rest of Europe. Jewish communities in France and Germany suffered from various discriminations and pressures, and if the situation in the peninsula seemed even more dramatic it was because Jews there had enjoyed relative freedom and partaken in the country's prosperity, influencing the economy and culture in an enviable manner.

Judaism has always retained within its collective memory Joseph's bitter experience. Joseph, son of Jacob, had been sold by his brothers and taken away to Egypt, where he became the pharaoh's court minion. Joseph then came to act as the protector and benefactor of his race, that is, until skinny cows replaced fat ones. When persecutions began the Jews had to leave the land of Egypt. The coincidence between recession and persecution can be considered a law of history according to the repetition of these cycles.[1] Such a law would be wholly confirmed by the tragic history of the Jews of Spain. During periods of expansion such as the twelfth and thirteenth centuries they experienced an extended period of progress and prosperity that was later idealized and turned into the myth of the existence of three cultures, medieval pluralism, and the golden age of Spanish Judaism. Nonetheless, no such pluralism actually existed; in fact, Jews were simply tolerated. Like the rest of their peninsular neighbors they benefited from the overall general prosperity of the times in political, military, demographic, and economic areas.[2] They were never, however, comparable to Christians. It was never forgotten that the implicit objective of the highest ecclesiastical authorities was to convert Jews and have them assimilate into the Christian religion and disappear as an autonomous community.

Two prevailing conditions were required for Jews to survive without encountering major problems with the rest of society: a healthy and prosperous economy and a state authority capable of guaranteeing the security of persons and possessions. In other words, the well-being of the Jews required a climate of economic expansion and political stability. These conditions were precisely those that were disappearing by the turn of the fourteenth century. The black plague and civil wars constituted crises experienced throughout Europe and made that century into one of the most dramatic in Spain's history. Jews suffered the effects of crisis not unlike Christians, but in addition economic difficulties increased insecurity and exacerbated conflict situations. The Scottish historian Angus MacKay has shown parallels and chronological coincidences between popular uprisings against Jews and converts and specific events such as price fluctuations, famines, and widespread misery during economic depression. Although MacKay's study focuses on the fifteenth century, his observations can be extended to other periods as well. Philippe Wolff, for example, arrives at similar conclusions for the crisis at the end of the fourteenth century in Catalonia and its consequences for the existence of the Catalonian aljamas.

The same can be said of political instability.[3] Jews themselves knew that very well. "Our lives and well-being depend upon the prosperity of the State under whose government we live," wrote Moses ha-Cohen de Tordesillas in 1375, referring to King Enrique II, and, he added, "This [king] is a refuge protecting us against all disasters."[4] The connection between the monarchy and Jews was more generalized than the privileged relationship between the king and a minority of court Jews who acted as financiers, tax collectors, or financial advisors for their sovereign. More than other groups, Jews supported a well-respected, strong state power to ensure public order and prevent or punish any type of disobedience or crime. Without that authority, Jews, due to their subordinate status, would be exposed to extortion, injustice, and personal and collective attack. Under such circumstances the general anti-Jewish sentiment, always latent among the general public, could become violent and function as an escape valve for internal societal tensions.

Medieval scholars tend to agree on the starting point of Spain's serious difficulties: the end of the thirteenth and the beginning of the fourteenth centuries, which had bad harvests, famines, scarcities, and inflationary spirals.[5] The plague in the middle of the fourteenth century resulted in a debilitated population incapable of resisting attacks of illness. The existing crisis situation was thus exacerbated and transformed into a veritable demographic catastrophe that in turn provoked a series of conflicts in medieval society. Peasants protested against the abusive demands of the *señores* (land-owning lords), who raised rents to compensate for lost income and also wanted to extend their territories and prerogatives in an attempt to reestablish feudalism. The monarchy clearly opposed this move because it was in the process of increasing its own control through a more efficient bureaucratic apparatus and a fiscal system that permitted it to meet political and wartime obligations.

During the second half of the fourteenth century this social conflict evolved into a civil war between Pedro I and his allies on the one hand and, on the other hand, some discontented sectors of the nobility grouped around Enrique de Trastámara.[6] As is known, the crisis ended with a change in dynasties that would have catastrophic consequences for the Jewish community. Hatred toward Jews, seen as responsible for causing misfortune, spread throughout fourteenth-century Europe. On the Iberian Peninsula there were three distinct areas, each corresponding to different political entities: Navarre, the Kingdom of Aragon, and Castile.

The Jewish communities of Navarre were rather well populated in the fourteenth century. The most significant were Tudela (more than a thousand individuals), Pamplona (some five hundred), and Estella (fewer than two hundred). As early as the last third of the thirteenth century, in 1277, the so-called revolt of the Navarrería occurred with the sacking of the Jewish neighborhood in Pamplona. Some fifty years later, in 1321, persecutions that also extended into Aragon were attributed to foreign elements, participants in the last crusades of the Pastorcillos from France, who murdered Jews in Jaca, Montclús, and Pamplona until Aragonese troops chased them away. The most serious insurrection occurred in Estella in 1328 at the death of the last sovereign of the French dynasty when a Franciscan monk incited the population to murder by overtly labeling Jews as Christ-slayers. Many Jews lost their lives, and others escaped from the city.[7]

Some twenty years later new insurrections occurred in Tudela, but this time Jews resisted with arms. On occasion these events led to the first Jewish conversions to Catholicism in the middle of the century. Nevertheless, Navarre returned to normalcy after those successively bloody years, and Jews were found once again in the textile trade, importing fabric from Flanders and England.[8] Under the reigns of Carlos II and Carlos III, aljamas recovered some of their former vitality and carried on, their existence unencumbered. The crown officially sanctioned their identity and autonomy. In 1390 King Carlos III created the office of *rab mayor,* naming his physician, Yosef Orabuena, to the post. Orabuena, who was responsible for representing all the aljamas and collecting a special tax contribution (the *pecha*) from them, held the office until his death in November of 1416.

The Jews of Navarre lived and worked as did all the king's subjects. Some were moneylenders who lent relatively small amounts on a short-term basis (six months to a year) at 25 percent interest. During this period Jews began to exercise a kind of monopoly in certain other financial activities, tax collecting for example. In 1383 the aljama of Estella, represented by Judas Leví, obtained a perpetual lease on the town's mills. That same man was also named official tax collector of Estella the previous year, a post generally held by a prominent townsman or cleric. Judas Leví was the first to hold the position from 1382 to 1388. As such, he was authorized to use the royal treasury to maintain fortifications on the border, maintain and perform work on castles, build major roads and bridges, and pay provincial officials' salaries. Within the peninsula, Navarre constituted a haven of peace for Castilian and Aragonese Jews who sought it out as a place of exile during the ordeals of 1391 and 1414.

In addition there were persecutions against Jews in the Kingdom of Aragon because of the plague of 1348. The poorer classes of society, due to religious fanaticism and superstition, considered Hebrews responsible for their misfortune and launched attacks against Jewish communities in various towns. Baer contends that only a fifth of the Jewish population of the Zaragoza community, one of the most significant Jewish areas, survived these attacks. In Barcelona and the northern areas of Catalonia similar attacks occurred but apparently with less loss of life. Approximately twenty people were killed, houses were destroyed, and financial records (such as payment slips and debt recognition papers) were burned. In Mallorca insurrections took place some time later, in 1374, with attacks against Jews accused of aggravating the famine, epidemics, and misery of the poor through their usurious loans to artisans and peasants. A first petition for the complete expulsion of Jews from the island was drafted at this time.

These popular revolts, despite their serious nature, did not actually endanger the existence of Aragonese Judaism. In these areas it was rare for popular hatred to be provoked and exploited by the wealthy who kept sight of their political objectives. The mendicant orders also made interventions, but these were less fanatic in character than those prevailing in Castile at the same time. In 1367 the Barcelona aljama was accused of buying sacred hosts, and an investigation was conducted that led to the indictment of three Jews who were then executed. During the trial the aljama as a whole was absolved of responsibility.

The Church's missionary campaign in the Kingdom of Aragon was not very systematic until the end of the century when the Franciscan Francesco Eiximenis wrote his great treatises full of anti-Jewish polemics. On the contrary, royal authorities attempted to prevent lawlessness by putting an end to such customs as those in Gerona, where Jews were traditionally assaulted during Holy Week. Local Christians would stone Jews and throw burning pieces of cloth into the Jewish quarter from the roof of the episcopal palace. In 1368 the king ordered the bishop to curb these abuses although we do not know how effective the results of this measure were. Throughout the century the parliament were not interested in the Jewish issue; only on one occasion was the problem of usury even mentioned. This was less of a matter of concern than in Castile because legal lending rates were kept at 20 percent. The participation of Jews in administration and politics, however, was such that it provoked much criticism and resentment.

It is important to emphasize that the principal cause for the favorable treatment of Jews was the relative neutrality of the wealthy and the existence of an indisputably strong royal power. These forces worked to remove all pretexts and politically motivated maneuvering to deflect discontent against Jews. According to Baer, with the end of the wars of Reconquest and colonization the political and economic role of specific groups of Jews declined as they were gradually distanced from high spheres of government. Christians could then compete effectively with Jews in both financial and governmental (political and administrative) spheres.

Generally speaking, the Aragonese Jew was a man of modest means, whether a shopkeeper, artisan, or farmer. The same was true of the typical Jew in Cata lonia. This is not to say there were not Jews in Barcelona who handled international trade with Valencia, Marseilles, and the Middle East or that there were not powerful families in Zaragosa like the Benveniste de la Caballería family. They and their Christian associates in Barcelona and Gerona participated in commercial affairs and, from 1380 on, were bankers and collectors of ecclesiastical rent for the Order of San Juan and the Archbishopric of Zaragosa. In 1361 another member of the family, Vidal, was entrusted with handling payments related to arming the cavalry, and in 1372 he held the lease for minting gold coins in partnership with the king's treasurer. The social position of the de la Caballería family in Zaragoza was exceptional. These were privileged Jews, and in the eyes of Christians as well. They were exonerated from paying taxes and uninvolved with governance of the aljama. In any case all Jewish communities in the Kingdom of Aragon enjoyed a comfortable situation compared to those in Castile during the same years. Baer also notes a certain degree of mutual tolerance and respect between Christian and Jewish intellectuals of similar cultural backgrounds and social status.

There are several ordinances related to the self-government of the aljamas dating from the fourteenth century. Those from 1327 and 1386 concerning Barcelona stipulated an organization with the following features: an integrated general assembly for the heads of families, executive officials, and economic, judicial and administrative powers. The direction of the aljama was the responsibility of a *Trentenari,* a college of thirty persons belonging to the most important lineages and renewed by thirds each year. A *Consell Estret* (restricted council) of eighteen members completed the organization. This oligarchic system was later extended to Valencia (1364) and Huesca (1374); the same family names reappeared in the forefront. Some sixty families directed Barcelona's aljama in the last decades of its existence. Of the sixty names, no fewer than fifteen figure on the lists of those baptized after the bloody events of 1391. "It is clear," comments Baer, "that these leaders of the Jewish community were attempting not to enter into the circle of martyrs."[9]

A royal order of 1377 curtailed part of the judicial autonomy of Barcelona's aljama. No longer would it be able to hand down death sentences or punishments such as amputations, nor was it allowed to judge matters between Christians and Jews. Instead, these types of complaints would be under the jurisdiction of a *baile* (bailiff), an official of the king. In all other areas, however, the aljama retained civil and criminal jurisdiction over its members. The fourteenth-century crisis, despite popular revolts, did not give rise to substantial changes for Jews in the Kingdom of Aragon. Rather, incidents in Castile had a contagious effect that led to the catastrophe during which Aragonese Judaism nearly disappeared.

In Castile throughout this period and until the height of terror during the year 1391 two themes nourished the masses' hatred of Jews: a series of unfounded rumors and the role attributed to Jews in handling money. The political opposition exploited popular resentment to the utmost. The fanaticism of some priests, based on the traditional anti-Judaism of the Church, did a great deal to instigate the killings of 1391.

Throughout Europe the epidemics generically known as the Black Plague reached their peak in 1348, unleashing a series of irrational rumors related to Jews' responsibility for the death toll. The idea was all the more absurd because Jews suffered from the plague as much as Christians did. Yet the panic gave way to uncontrolled reactions in Germany, where groups of disciplinarians ran through the streets, beating their flesh and attacking Jews to placate the wrath of God.[10] Perhaps the most widespread rumor was that the plague was being spread by way of well water that Jews had deliberately poisoned.[11] In 1321 several Jews and lepers were burned in France because of false documents supposedly testifying that the Jews of Toledo had consorted with other Jews in France and with the Moors in Granada and Morocco to poison the water Christians drank. In Teruel, also in 1321, a Christian was accused of poisoning the water; under torture he declared that he had acted at the instigation of Jews.[12]

A population disoriented by the implacable and inexplicable death toll, acute food shortages, and enormous price hikes credulously ingested such rumors. This situation in turn provoked social tensions between rich and poor, lords and vassals, taxpayers and the royal palace. Various historians rightfully interpret the prevailing context in which hatred against Jews was exacerbated as episodes of social unrest that erupted at specific intervals. Nonetheless, priests' defense of the anti-Jewish thesis in their diatribes over the years laid the groundwork. All these factors concurred to make Jews into the incarnation of absolute evil, those whose presence unleashed the wrath of the Almighty.

"Here come the Jews, ready to drink the blood of the poor and wretched." With that phrase the chancellor López de Ayala summed up the quintessence of popular anti-Judaism. It is easy to understand why conflicts would be sharpened over money matters during a crisis. Money to buy bread and basic goods was lacking, and given the drought and bad harvests prices reached exorbitant levels. Money was lacking to pay rent to secular and religious property owners all the more demanding in their attempts to alleviate their own suffering due to the effects of the crisis. Money was also lacking to pay increasingly onerous taxes. For all of these reasons people were borrowing scarce money at high rates of interest. Here is where we encounter the figures of the Jewish moneylender and fiscal agent.

It is clear that not all Jews—indeed, few—corresponded to these stereotypes. That some were exercising these money-handling roles was enough, however, to fuel popular anger against Jews, who appeared to both cause the misery and benefit from it. The theme of usury then moved to the forefront. The Church prohibited Christians from lending at interest, considering it an illicit way to earn a living. In other words, although the Church did not censure large credit operations it banned money-lending against gages and therefore claimed to defend the poor against not princes and lords but usurers.[13]

It is true that any society has difficulty existing without credit, including during periods of growth and expansion. Credit allows for improved profits in various industries, especially in agriculture where it facilitates land acquisition, breaking new ground, and purchasing tools or grain. Some Jews were thus led to handle money matters not from natural inclination but to fulfill a social function—nothing more, nothing less.[14] Those Jews involved in lending money and collecting taxes or rents played a role that was complementary to the economic activities of Christians, but money matters were still not a Jewish specialization or propensity. It is important to abandon once and for all the overused argument that Jews were the only initiators of capitalism due to their unique ability to manage money.

It is true that money was becoming scarce in Castile and was therefore lent at a very high interest rate, 33.3 percent by the end of the thirteenth century. Any interest rate above that was considered to be usury, a practice punishable by law. Loans were not prohibited, not even loans with interest, but usurious loans that included charging interest above the legal rate were. It is therefore not very precise to speak in terms of Jewish usury for the problem during the fourteenth century was much more one of Jewish debt. Debtors claimed that loans held by Jews were usurious in order to avoid making payments on them. As lenders were forewarned, they took precautions such as requiring collateral of a higher value than the amount of the loan or covering interest beforehand so only the principal of a debt would be recorded. These practices were indeed "frauds of usury," prohibited and punishable by law. The most frequent accusations against Jewish lenders were motivated by a desire to have loans dismissed and be able to denounce Jews legally. The myth of the Jewish usurer, exploiter of the people, had been born. This character was to become the main protagonist in the crisis, and all Jews were lumped together to become the recipients of overwhelming resentment.

Alfonso XI attempted to remedy the situation and pacify passions that were heating up by prohibiting Jews from acting as lenders altogether. That was the objective of the Order of Alcala, passed by the parliament in 1348, which stated that Jews were to change profession and become farmers and that they were to be facilitated in acquiring fertile land for that purpose. Such a decision showed great initiative on the part of the king; the judges only required the abolishment of part of the debts previously contracted. The objective of the Order of Alcala was to equate Jews and Christians. It was an invitation for some Jews involved in money lending to change their way of making a living so they would no longer be differentiated from Christians in any visible way, at least not due to their mode of subsistence. Alfonso XI's law was not enacted; perhaps it came too late, but it allows us to see how a respected royal power might have been able to redress a trend and reorient political economics in the right direction. What occurred after the king's death confirms this observation.

The political crisis in Castile was latent as of the end of the thirteenth century. A few anxious nobles opposed royal power to obtain new privileges. As soon as Alfonso XI reached legal age in 1325 he worked efficiently to reform the crown's relationship with the nobles. He needed to initiate economic and fiscal policies to support international trade, the development of cattle raising, and the export of merino wool. The taxes on transactions (*alcabala*) in royal rents began to represent more income than the taxes voted in the parliament, which gave the monarch much more autonomy and scope for action. In municipalities the substitution of open councils for closed regimes (1345) and the naming of royal correctors in the main cities (1348) were an important step toward centralization. Such politics favored consensus among commercial interests, the bourgeoisie, and the cities but discontented the land-holding noble class, which saw its hopes dashed.

In succeeding his father in 1350 Pedro I gave the impression that he would continue promoting the same centralism and authoritarianism of the previous reign. He was aided by scholars trained in Roman law from the urban middle class and did not rely on Jewish elements. In 1351 he ordered the creation of the *Becerro de las Behetrías* (Register of Privileges and Nobility of Freely Elected Lordships), a detailed investigation to better delineate the fiscal and territorial rights of nobles and thus restrict the extension of secular and religious dominions. Pedro I then clashed with magnates led by Albuquerque, Alfonso XI's former minion, and Alfonso XI's illegitimate son Don Enrique, the Count of Trastámara.

The military losses suffered by the nobles in 1353, 1355, and 1356 along with the exile of some of the most compromised among them allowed Pedro I to maintain relative peace in the kingdom until 1366. In that year Enrique de Trastámara received aid not only from France but also from the papacy and from Aragon, both generous in economic and military support. The famous White Companies of French and English mercenaries led by Captain Bertrand du Guesclin attacked Castile to sustain Enrique's claims. The crisis degenerated into a civil war lasting three years and ending with the death of Pedro I, assassinated in Montiel in 1369, and the ascension of a new dynasty, that of the Trastámaras.

From the beginning, the Count of Trastámara's followers manipulated the Jewish issue to discredit Pedro I and make him unpopular with the people. As early as 1351 they forced the king to prevent Jews from lending money by practicing usury. The honorific conferred upon Samuel ha-Leví, named royal treasurer in 1353, was considered to be a provocation. Immensely wealthy— having built both Toledo's temple, the *sinagoga del Tránsito,* and the palace today known as the Casa del Greco—Samuel ha-Leví offered his business and diplomatic services to sovereign powers, thus renewing the tradition of court Jews collaborating with monarchs be they Muslim or Christian. Many other Jews also held positions as tax or royal rent collectors.

Jews, both court bureaucrats and fiscal agents, thus appeared from a certain point of view as the most significant element of growing royal power. Because Jews maintained their habitual loyalty and adherence to the legitimate power it was easy to attack the monarchy's connection—when indeed it was not its subordination—to Jews. Occasionally, some Jews gave the impression of wielding great influence over the sovereign and society in general. At the inauguration of the synagogue Samuel ha-Leví was self-congratulatory in remarking on the excellent life enjoyed by Castilian Jews under Pedro I's protection. In Trastámara's propaganda, however, Pedro I was consistently portrayed as the protector of the Jews and as such as their accomplice in the unholy exploitation of the people. It was rumored that Pedro I was not the son of King Alfonso XI but rather the son of Pero Gil.[15] Gil was a Jew who reportedly had managed to succeed with the ingenious and incredible scheme of substituting his newborn son [who became Pedro I] for the baby girl who was the legitimate offspring of the royal marriage.

The consequence of this campaign was the resurgence of anti-Jewish insurrections in Castile. The first transgression occurred in 1355 when Enrique's troops entered Toledo. On this occasion soldiers, not townspeople, launched the attack against Jewish neighborhoods. Ten years later when the civil war broke out things took a much more systematic turn. A document from 1366 presents Pedro I as the king who "was promoting and enriching the Moors and Jews and making them into lords."[16] Upon entering Burgos in April 1366, Don Enrique demanded the enormous sum of 1 million *maravedís* from the Jews, threatening to sell as slaves those who could not pay their share. In the spring of 1367 French mercenaries led by Du Guesclin razed the Jewish community of Briviesca. In the fall of the same year the population of Valladolid attacked the Jewish community with the battle cry "long live King Don Enrique!" Although there were no casualties, eight synagogues were sacked. In all areas the civil war led to the ruin and demoralization of the aljamas while popular hatred of the Jews was rife and began to wield short- and long-term effects.

As soon as Enrique II was crowned, in 1369, he softened his attitude and acted less violently toward Jews. This was, moreover, a matter of expedience given the monarchy's interests. He had nonetheless planted the seeds of hatred that would bear bloody fruit before the end of the century, and the course politics was about to take was evident. In June of 1369 Don Enrique forced Toledo's Jews to sell their belongings at public auction for an amount of 20,000 *doblas* of gold.[17] One of the first orders he dictated concerned a general moratorium on Jewish debts. That act prompted Christians in Segovia and Avila to attack Jewish homes, robbing and destroying the debtors' notes and mortgages. According to the Court of Soria (1380), the aljamas were no longer allowed to judge penal matters punishable by death sentences, amputation, or exile. The Jews remained authorized, however, to judge civil complaints among members of their own community and to select one of the Christian judges who came to preside in criminal matters. These matters could be appealed before a royal court. In other matters Enrique II returned to a politics more in line with tradition. He once again entrusted the Jews with the task of tax collecting. He also named a number of Jews as chief auditors, but on the whole the role of Jews was no longer as relevant as it had once been. In Ladero Quesada's opinion, although they were still tax collectors Jews in no way held any monopoly as collectors of royal rents, and by the time of Enrique II's reign very few were left who still held high positions in the royal court.

The civil war and Trastámara's victory were great blows to Castilian Judaism.

According to fiscal records there were only four large aljamas toward the end of the fourteenth century in Toledo, Burgos, Seville, and Murcia. There were also several medium-sized Jewish communities such as those in Aguilar de Campo or Alcala de Henares, and very small aljamas were dispersed throughout Castile. These were in no way homogeneous communities. Although some individuals were very rich the overwhelming majority of Jews were of humble origins and modest condition. Trastámara's propaganda aimed at stating the contrary so it would be understood that Jews had come to form a socially privileged group in terms of wealth. Most serious of all, the hatred felt toward Jews had changed in nature. No longer was it a simple aversion for a sect that did not admit Jesus as the Messiah. Religious factors had begun to be used in an ideological way in social and political conflicts. From this point on, Jews were designated as the guilty party for all misfortunes that befell people. The catastrophe that occurred at the end of the fourteenth century ultimately confirmed that the Jewish issue could efficiently be used by politicians who had bad intentions.

3

The Convert Problem
(1391–1474)

The 1391 Killings

Between 1391 and 1416 the position of Spanish Jews changed radically. Nevertheless, it would be an exaggeration to refer to it as a "final solution, prepared for in a legal and emotional way."[1] That kind of vocabulary corresponds to another period of history, that of Hitlerian totalitarianism, and I do not believe it is appropriate in understanding the period examined herein. What is certain is that in the years between 1391 and 1416 a new society was created with the emergence of a significant minority of converts and that new situation, in the long run, led to the Inquisition and the expulsion of 1492.

Américo Castro stated that he saw in the events of 1391 a point of no return in the reversal of Spain's Hebrew community. That year signaled in and of itself the end of an era of tolerance and the beginning of the "age of conflict." He is, however, mistaken in his attempt to find causes for such a warped destiny. Not everything can be explained by the fanaticism of frenzied priests. It is true that some preachers' sermons enraged the Christian masses and incited them to commit murder. Yet preachers were demagogically exploiting a preexisting crisis complicated by political difficulties.[2] This is clear given what occurred in Catalonia and Mallorca. In Barcelona the *poble menut* (little people), sailors and fishermen, asked help from farmers to attack the Jewish quarter. It was said that the "great" wanted to destroy the "small," and burning the houses of the wealthy was mentioned.[3] In Gerona there were similar occurrences, and those who sacked the Jewish quarters were poor farmers.[4] In Palma events began with the revolt of the poor against the *grossos* (wealthy) and ended with the murder of Jews.

The observation can be extended throughout Spain. In all areas unrest was spreading, unleashing a terrible class war. The authorities—representatives of the king and nobles—attempted to oppose this violence, but the only result was to aggravate it.[5] In this case as in so many others in history, ideology—religious anti-Judaism—masked socioeconomic motives. The "other"—that is, the one who does not share the same faith as the masses—is considered responsible for all society's misfortunes. The contrast between the misery of the people and the prosperity of a few Jews seemed scandalous. Social hatred of the rich converted into religious hatred of non-Catholics.

Provoked by religious fanaticism, anti-Jewish violence erupted. One of the circumstances that contributed to its spread, at least in Castile, was the void in power created by the death of Juan I in October 1390. In view of Enrique III's youth it was necessary to form a regency council, but that body proved incapable of agreeing on matters of government. All of this is summarized in a few extraordinarily lucid sentences by López de Ayala, the royal chancellor:

> The townspeople did not have any regard for the king's orders concerning the cities. Some reacted because of the sermons, others out of a desire to rob and others because they had no fear of the king. Given the sovereign's youth and the discord among the lords of the kingdom regarding the testament [of Juan I] and the Council, they could not respect the king's letters, nor the orders of towns or gentlemen; for this, things turned out badly. All this was motivated by a license to rob [continued the chancellor] according to what seemed to be the case—more than a matter of faith or devotion.[6]

It all began in Seville. As early as 1378 the Archdeacon of Ecija, Fernán Martínez, initiated a campaign of provocative sermons against the Jewish community. He advocated cutting off all relations with Jews and destroying their synagogues or transforming them into churches. Fernán Martínez, however, was speaking in his own name. The Catholic hierarchy had taken away his authority, and by 1382 the archbishop of Seville, Pedro Gómez Barroso, alerted Juan I to the problem of the archdeacon's incendiary oratory.

Martínez did not heed the king's orders. On the contrary, he began to be protected by a small group of determined men. Even after two more warnings from the king in 1388 he did not back down. These written warnings were, in truth, rather imprudent: Jews should not be mistreated "in spite of the fact that they are evil and perverse." Juan I added, "If you wish to be a good Christian, be one in your house, better that than run after Jews in this way."[7]

In 1389 the archbishop decided to put an end to the archdeacon's disobedience. He was prohibited from preaching from then on and from mentioning the Jewish issue under penalty of excommunication. On July 7 of the following year, however, Archbishop Barroso died. Fernán Martínez, who had an official role as provisor, then became the administrator with the highest authority in the now-vacant diocese of Seville. A short time later the king died. The Archdeacon of Ecija was free to do what he wanted. No political or ecclesiastical power could prevent him from acting out his whims and fantasies. He did not waste time implementing his theories and ordered the defilement of synagogues in the city and the confiscation of Jewish prayer books. He also continued with his incendiary preaching.

The first bloody revolt took place in January 1391. The constable (*alguacil mayor*) of Seville, Alvar Pérez de Guzmán, Count of Niebla, and other municipal officials managed to snuff it out and punish instigators by hanging them. Yet the regency council dismissed these officers and appointed new ones. Martínez was feeling all-powerful, and on June 6 he sent his men into the Jewish ghettos. Two synagogues were converted into churches, and others were burned. Above all, the revolt caused the death of some four hundred people in the Jewish community. That figure is perhaps inflated, but it gives an idea of the horror the events caused—sacking, pillaging, burning, and killing.

The violence spread beyond Seville to Alcalá de Guadaira, Carmona, Ecija, and Santa Olalla. From southern Andalusia it moved by mid June to Córdoba, Andujar, Ubeda, and Baeza. In all those towns anti-Jewish insurrections occurred, and not all of them were spontaneous; they entailed murders, robberies, sacking, and burning. The wave of violence soon hit areas close to Ciudad Real, Toledo, and Cuenca. In the northern plateaus of Castile the situation was somewhat less dramatic. Rioters seemed to be limiting themselves to sacking the neighborhoods and homes of Jews without resorting to the murders that had bloodied the south. No serious incidents are recorded for Burgos or Navarre.[8]

In the Kingdom of Aragon, Zaragoza escaped the killings as well. In Valencia, however, the disturbances began early in July. Martín, brother and heir to the king, was incapable of preventing the attacks on the Jewish community. Some two hundred people were murdered. In addition, there were rapes as well as robberies and pillaging, and many houses were set on fire. In Gerona the authorities took measures to prevent violence and detained some leaders. The Count of Ampurias offered refuge to Jews in his castle, and all and all the storm caused relatively little damage. The same was true in Tortosa and Perpignan. In Lérida, however, where the castle was attacked, the number of victims reached seventy-eight. In Barcelona the attack against Jews began in early August, and again there were murders and fires as well as looting. In Mallorca around the same time the governor general advised Jews to seek refuge in Palma, where he felt he could defend them more effectively. His precautions turned out to be useless, however, given that rioters could count on the complicity of the bailiff, who would later be sentenced to death and executed. In any event more than three hundred people lost their lives.

Never had violence against Jews gone so far, and they were horrified at events. Some families in Mallorca, for example, decided to leave the Spanish kingdoms. They went to North Africa, heading for Tripoli, Tunis, Argel, Oran, or Marrakech. Many more Jews (perhaps some hundred thousand) decided to renounce their faith and convert, either spontaneously or under threat in order to protect themselves and their families from new persecutions. The conversions gave an extraordinary lift to a movement begun years earlier. In Valladolid, for example, the first conversions of Jews to Christianity took place between 1370 and 1380. In the Kingdom of Aragon, Isaac Golluf asked for baptism in August 1389 and renamed himself Juan Sánchez de Calatayud.[9] Perhaps one of the most famous converts at the end of the fourteenth century was Salomón ha-Leví, the *rabí mayor* of Burgos. He was probably baptized in July 1390, a year before the massive killings took place.[10] When he became a Christian he took the name Pablo de Santa María inasmuch as he claimed, as a member of the Leví tribe, to be related to the Virgin Mary.[11] He ultimately became bishop of Burgos.[12]

In fact, it is probable that some Jews had thought about renouncing their faith for some time. Yitzhak Baer and Léon Poliakov believe that thoughts of conversion were current among the social and intellectual elite. For some, "the conversion to Catholicism began as something of a political calculation designed to provide an 'admission ticket' into the secular world for a career in civil service and the state bureaucracy."[13] Others such as rabbis converted to Catholicism because they did not find adequate responses in Judaism for their religious skepticism. That might very well have been the case for Salomón ha-Leví, who justified his conduct by citing works by such authors as Maimonides, Saint Thomas, Ramón Martí, and Abner de Burgos. In his book *Or Adonai* (Light of the Lord), Hasday Abraham Crescas (1340–1410) of Zaragoza accused certain Jews of rationalism, the result of reading too much Aristotle.[14]

Nevertheless, the overwhelming majority of converts in 1391 were obeying less intellectual impulses. It was terror that convinced them to make the move. The royal and Church authorities, although they had officially condemned the violence, regarded conversion as an opportunity to diminish the number of Jews. They considered conversions to be valid and acted to broaden the movement initiated in 1391 through less drastic but not less efficient means. I am referring to the legal methods that were employed to isolate the Jewish community and the proselytizing of those years.

At the beginning of the fifteenth century in Castile several measures were aimed at definitively prohibiting Jewish usury (the Order of 1405). Yet the Ayllon laws (1412), promulgated by Queen Doña Catalina during the minority of Juan II with the support of Pablo de Santa María and possibly due to the influence of Vincente Ferrer, constituted a milestone in the legal discrimination against Jews. The measures contemplate the "enclosure of the Jews and of the Moors," but the former were the primary victims. The judicial autonomy the aljamas had previously enjoyed was eliminated. A list of occupations Jews were forbidden to practice was published and included physician, storekeeper, tax collector, blacksmith, carpenter, tailor, cloth-shearer, butcher, furrier, and shoemaker. Jews were no longer allowed to use the title *don* and were obliged to wear a beard and long hair so they could easily be distinguished from Christians. They were also instructed to wear on top of their clothing—which had to be modest and not luxurious—a red shield (the *rodela bermeja*). The most serious measure, which introduced the most radical change for Jews, was the obligation to live in exclusively separate and gated neighborhoods from which they were only allowed to leave under certain conditions. From this point on *juderías* (separate Jewish communities) began to form in different cities. Thus Jews lost the right to freely change their residences.

It is clear that the laws were attempting to make life so difficult for Jews that they would want to convert. In 1414 laws similar to Castile's Ayllon laws were promulgated in the Kingdom of Aragon, albeit with one additional aggravating measure. It would now be illegal to have more than one synagogue per aljama and possess the Talmud. Moreover, the Jews of the Kingdom of Aragon were obliged to listen to three sermons a year: on the second Sunday of Advent, Easter Monday, and a third to be designated by the local authority. This last measure clarified the others. The crown and the Church were working in tandem toward the same goal—the conversion of Jews, with the catechism complementing legal measures.

This collaboration was evident in the Kingdom of Aragon, where the famous Debate of Tortosa (1413) took place. The purpose of the debate was to convince Jews that the Messiah had indeed arrived and that rabbis had deliberately falsified the Talmud to hide that fact. This would be reason enough for Jews to renounce their false beliefs and embrace Catholicism. It was not the first time demonstrations of this type had been arranged. In 1263 the Dominicans had organized one in Barcelona and denounced Hebrew books for phrases injurious to Christianity and doctrinal falsifications. Yet the Debate of Tortosa had a distinctive character for it took place in an atmosphere of heightened anti-Jewish tensions immediately after the killings of 1391 and during a period in which legal discrimination against Jews was being reinforced. Pope Benedict XIII, perhaps influenced by the convert Jerónimo de Santa Fe, launched the initiative. As almost always occurs in these cases, neophytes were sometimes more fervent in their desire to proselytize.

The very name *debate* or *dispute* (as it was called in Spanish, the *disputa de Tortosa*) is dubious. In Tortosa there was no real debate or free discussion regarding the interpretation of the Holy Scriptures and doctrinal aspects of both religions. The fourteen rabbis who participated in the meeting had to be very circumspect about introducing certain themes in order to avoid being accused of attacking Christianity. They had to limit themselves to questions, asking for clarifications and explanations in a respectful tone before an audience of fellow Jews also subject to the same conditions. The Jews were obliged to leave their jobs in order to attend this ceremony; essentially, they had been summoned to witness the intellectual humiliation of their rabbis. After suffering this humiliation, the rabbis attempted to discuss matters and defend their positions, but the pope suspended the sessions. He did not wish the debate to be transformed into a controversy because he had created the occasion to force the rabbis into a public confession of their errors and the stubbornness of their beliefs.

The name of Vicente Ferrer is inextricably linked to the proselytizing of those years. He constantly repeated that he was against all violence and that the only conversions he promoted were those that occurred spontaneously, that is, when a convinced infidel living in error requested of his own free will to become part of the Church. Although there is no reason to doubt these declarations, Vincente knew very well how to exploit lay officials, for example, by having them require Jews to listen to his sermons regardless of their wishes. His apostolate began before 1391 but did not have much impact until after 1407. Thanks to his good relationships with the Luna pope, Benedict XIII, and with the *infante*, Don Fernando de Antequera, who supported him in a decisive manner, he became the king of Aragon (Compromise of Caspe, 1412). In other words, given his reliance on help from political powers, Vicente Ferrer's parish was not just a religious endeavor. Moreover, he did not limit his activities to the Kingdom of Aragon; he also became extremely involved in Castilian affairs.[15]

Under these circumstances it is not very surprising that numerous conversions took place, among them those of fourteen rabbis who had participated in the Debate of Tortosa as well as the De la Caballería clan, a prominent Jewish family in Zaragoza.[16] Very few of the conversions were sincere given the political, social, and ideological pressure exerted on Jews during the years from 1391 to 1415. There were popular uprisings against Jews around 1413–14 such as the one that occurred in Daroca. The infante Don Alfonso gave orders that no violence should be waged against Jews, adding that forced conversions pleased neither God nor the king.

That was the theory. The reality was very different. Fearful, demoralized because of the persecutions and the apostasy of its elite, many Jews thus converted to Christianity in both the Kingdom of Aragon and in Castile.[17] What happened during this period was a first attempt at massive conversion, one that anticipated the intensive Catholic proselytizing at the end of the fifteenth century in Seville during the months preceding the establishment of the Inquisition and then throughout Spain after publication of the expulsion edict in 1492. Judaism chronicles the year 1391 as one of persecutions and oppression but 1414 as the year of apostasy.[18] Thus, between 1391 and 1415 a new category in the religious geography of the peninsula was created—converts or new Christians. The idea had been to put an end to Judaism, but a new problem with widespread and dramatic ramifications—that of the convert—was created in the process.

Spanish Judaism in the Fifteenth Century

The tragic events of 1391 and the militant catechism of 1413–14 had significantly changed the number of Jews in the peninsula. After the mass of conversions (perhaps a hundred thousand) the Hebrew community was not able to recover. It emerged from the crisis not only physically diminished but also morally and intellectually destroyed. The geography of peninsular Judaism had been completely transformed. Major aljamas disappeared in the Kingdom of Aragon, notably in Valencia and Barcelona. Only thirty-five such institutions survived: one in Palma de Mallorca, five in the Kingdom of Valencia, and those in Murviedro and Castellón. Among them were eight in Catalonia, including small communities in Lérida, Gerona, and Cervera, and twenty-two in the Kingdom of Aragon, which suffered less in the upheaval.

The aljama of Zaragoza still numbered about two hundred families and was distinguished by its relative prosperity owing to involvement in cloth manufacture, merchandising, and, especially, medicine. Smaller-scale aljamas could be found in Huesca, Calatayud, Tarazona, Daroca, Teruel, Monzón, Egea, Jaca, and Barbastro. At the time of the expulsion in 1492 the Jewish population of the Kingdom of Aragon amounted to no more than six thousand families, fewer, that is, than fifty thousand individuals. According to Baer, this reduction and dispersion had a double purpose—on one hand the displacement of Jews from the Kingdom of Aragon to the Kingdom of Castile and on the other the tendency to abandon large cities and settle in smaller towns thought less exposed to Christian repression.

In the Kingdom of Castile the most telling fact was the decline of the great urban Jewish communities of the south. Andalusia was transformed into an area teeming with converts. Northern Castile had been less affected by the violent events of 1391, and it held on to several important Jewish communities.[19] Here too, however, as in the Kingdom of Aragon, a marked dispersion took place. The hundred thousand Jews living in the Castilian territories divided into more than two hundred aljamas and tended to regroup in small towns and even rural areas. In Toledo, regarded as the capital of Castilian Judaism in the previous century, only forty Hebrew families stayed on. Conversely, Judaism flourished in Talavera de la Reina. Segovia also experienced a wave of conversions, and in Valladolid the number of Jews steadily diminished throughout the fifteenth century, declining to about a thousand individuals in 1480. There were even fewer Jews in Burgos (perhaps twenty families) than in small villages like Torrelaguna or Haro (fifty families). Finally, the Jewish population grew in towns under seignorial jurisdiction, among them Hita, Buitrago, Cuellar, and Plasencia.

The tension that had characterized the last years of the fourteenth century and the first years of the fifteenth subsided after 1420. Pope Martin V proved less intransigent than Benedict XIII. In addition, both Juan II of Castile and Alfonso V of Aragon tended to relax some of the repressive measures of the *Ordenamiento de Ayllón,* so much so that some of its harsher measures fell into disuse. Once again Jews could attend synagogue and use religious books that had been confiscated. They returned to occupations they had been prohibited from exercising. The rules requiring them to attend sermons were relaxed as were those requiring them to wear the distinctive *rodela bermeja.*

The Hebrew community felt the need to rebuild its internal organization and resume its religious activities. The assembly of Valladolid celebrated in 1432 was a response to this. The representatives of the aljamas of Castile, with Abraham Benveniste presiding, developed laws establishing new norms for their internal government. The king sanctioned their decisions in 1432 in an act that had great implications because in doing so he symbolically recognized the legal and autonomous existence of the Jewish community of Castile as an integral part of the kingdom although it was still inferior to the Christian community. He thus broke with the plan instituted during the period from 1391 to 1415 of assimilating Jews by force. The Kingdom of Castile returned to official acceptance of the idea that a minority of its subjects practiced a religion other than Christianity. Furthermore, it recognized the right of this minority as a legal entity with its own laws.

The aljamas thus recovered judicial autonomy, with the power to judge and punish according to their own laws those Jews who violated regulations. The only difference was that aljamas no longer were allowed to condemn criminals to death. Instead, they were limited to banishing such malefactors from the community. Likewise, aljamas obtained the right to collect special taxes to maintain Jewish schools and places of worship. In this way they were able to reconstruct the Jewish community with the crown's blessing. Representatives of aljamas were to meet periodically to deal with such matters of common concern to the Jewish population as taxes and legal and other religious or political issues. Abraham Benveniste was named the rab of the court and as such was to wield authority over all Jews in the kingdom. He came to exercise a double mandate. On one hand he represented the aljamas before the king and on the other he at the same time acted as the king's delegate before other Jews.

Reorganized along these lines, the Hebrew community of Castile rebuilt itself although it would never again experience the splendor of previous eras. Rabbinical and theological studies testify to its intellectual vitality. Throughout the fifteenth century several works of biblical exegesis (editions, translations, and commentaries) were produced.[20] On occasion these attracted the attention of Christian university scholars. Among them, for example, is the *Biblia de la casa de Alba* (Bible of the House of Alba), with a Castilian translation and notes by Rabbi Moses Arragel de Guadalajara, a work done at the behest of the master of Calatrava, Don Luis de Guzmán, between 1422 and 1433 with the collaboration of the Franciscans of Toledo. On occasion, there is the impression of a return to the convivencia of times past. Baer cites the case of Cuellar, during the 1470s, when some Christians attended the celebration of Yom Kippur and went to the synagogue to hear the sermons of Rabbi Simmel, a celebrated physician and philosopher.[21]

The reconstruction of the aljamas, however, should not obscure from memory the overwhelming degradation suffered by peninsular Judaism due to the apostasy of a large number of its practitioners. Many Jews became the sworn enemies of converts, whom they considered as traitors and renegades. Likewise, converts harbored animosity against those who espoused their former religion. That enmity is one of the various aspects of the convert issue that became the key problem within Castilian society.

The Convert Problem

During the fifteenth century Jews slipped into the background; *cristianos nuevos* (new Christians) or *conversos* (converts) now constituted the major political, social, and religious problem. How many people became Christians due to the persecutions of 1391 and those that followed? There were probably fewer than two hundred thousand people, less than 5 percent of the total population of Spain. Although converts thus constituted a minority, it was concentrated in urban centers and therefore attracted a great deal of attention. Moreover, they were not a socially homogeneous group. They did not make up a social class or demonstrate many signs of group solidarity. As Miguel Ángel Ladero Quesada has indicated, converts did not demonstrate clear signs of the kind of endogamy to maintain group identity.[22] It is possible, as Hernando de Pulgar, the fifteenth-century converso, has suggested, that converted women demonstrated greater endogamy among themselves.[23]

Nonetheless, Pulgar's observation has been challenged by numerous instances of female converts marrying traditional Christians. Mixed marriages—Christian men who married converted women and converted men who married Christian women—were apparently quite commonplace. That is why gathering information on the "purity of blood" in the following century was a tedious and terrible business that had to be carried back two generations to see if there was Jewish blood among grandparents. In essence, the converts' originality was that, generally, they managed complete assimilation into the rest of Christian society and were able to erase what most of their new coreligionists considered to be shameful origins.

The converts' tragic destiny was that of a category of people wanting to assimilate but ultimately rejected by the "old Christians." Converts, for new Christians, remained Jews despite baptism, complicated by the fact that as Christians they could have responsibilities, honors, and offices previously denied by their former religion. For the most part, members of the Jewish social elite of the aljamas were likely to convert, sometimes following a move initiated by the leading rabbis.

Converts were, on the whole, better-educated people with higher cultural levels. Under these circumstances it is logical that converts held relevant positions in both the monastic and nonmonastic clergy. The former rabbi from Burgos, Salomón ha-Leví, after his baptism returned to that city as bishop using his new Christian name, Pablo de Santa María. The same type of conversions existed in other sectors of society. Initially, converts no longer suffered from legal discriminations that had barred Jews' access to certain positions of authority in directing public affairs or in administration. Moreover, thanks to research conducted by Francisco Márquez Villanueva, we are better informed about the growing numbers of converts in councils and local governments (*regimientos*) throughout the fifteenth century.[24] This was, for example, when families such as the Santa Marías, the Maluendas, and the Cartagenas came to occupy leading positions in the city council of Burgos.[25]

The converts' social success was what provoked ire, rancor, and hatred. For the common people, converts were forever and indelibly marked by their origins, and that attitude grew into racism. The average citizen suspected that the conversions had not been sincere and that many new Christians secretly practiced their former religion and maintained its rituals. Generally speaking, the accusation was unfounded although it would be more precise to nuance it, distinguishing religious practices from those of a more sociological or cultural nature. Maintaining certain eating habits, for example, does not necessarily have religious significance in and of itself and does not contradict sincere faith in Church dogma. It is difficult to change habits practiced since childhood. As Andrés Bernáldez stated at the end of the century, it is easier to change beliefs than a way of living. To renounce that would be like death. Moreover, given the scarce or nonexistent religious instruction converts usually received at the time of baptism, how could they be required to become perfect Catholics from the start? Such questions preoccupied a certain class of individuals when the idea took hold to create an inquisition to punish bad Christians and converts who publicly claimed to be Christians yet practiced Jewish rituals in secret.

In reality, some converts' skepticism and notorious lack of religious belief complicated the problem. It could be said that these individuals were in practice neither Catholics nor Jews. This is what Francisco Márquez Villanueva called "the weight of the Saduccean attitude . . . that negates the immortality of the soul and tends to see in law a material alliance, aimed at obtaining only earthly possessions."[26] Despite becoming Christians those Jews remained ambiguous and disdainful of representations and religious rituals they considered good for the ignorant and vulgar masses alone. That perception allowed many Jews to convert to Christianity, for it was all the same to them to be part of one religion or another. Judaism had only created problems for them, whereas conversion facilitated life and allowed them to become involved in more areas of society without the obstacles posed by legal discrimination that barred access to specific positions. Thus, in a society so deeply impregnated with religious values, where religion was closely linked to all aspects of daily life, this absence of religious faith came to represent a kind of scandal; it was a revolt against popular sentiment and contributed to reinforcing resentment against converts.

Such religious tensions were behind the true form of the convert problem in fifteenth-century Spain and led to the creation of a latent climate of hostility against Jews and converts that was ready to be carried to violent extremes in the event of political or social crisis. As mentioned, a kind of general law was being repeated—the correlation between crisis situations and religious persecution. Events of the fifteenth century confirmed that correlation.

As of the 1420s, a return to normalcy lasted through the middle of the century, and Jews once again reclaimed their status. They were guaranteed an autonomous existence within the kingdom in exchange for a higher fiscal burden compared to Christians and had to submit to various discriminations not always applied in a strict manner. In Castile, Álvaro de Luna attempted to establish order and reestablish the crown's authority over various groups of nobles. As always, Jews were convinced that only strong state power could guarantee their security, and they therefore offered to serve Álvaro de Luna.

Consequently, nobles opposed those politics that tended to reinforce royal power and were decidedly anti-Jewish and later anti-convert. That position allowed them to weaken the monarchy and at the same time attract partisans from the masses with their demagogical stances. Abraham Benveniste, for whom the post of rab mayor was reestablished in the kingdom, was the key figure among Jewish supporters of the crown. Considered a great expert in finance, he was responsible for the collection of all taxes. To that end, the mercantile company Abraham Benveniste formed in 1431 to handle tax collection was composed mainly of Christians.

Fiscal problems again exacerbated anti-Jewish sentiments. In early 1449 Álvaro de Luna decided to add an additional tax to the city of Toledo's burden: a forced loan of a million *maravedís,* the collection of which was entrusted to a convert named Alonso de Cota. This bad news provoked general discontent and ended in the popular revolt of January 26, 1449. Álvaro de Luna's adversaries—among them groups of nobles and the heir to the throne, Don Enrique (the future King Enrique IV)—took advantage of the opportunity to attack the prevailing political structure and overturn it. Pero Sarmiento, the governor of the castle, was ready to support their plans. Sarmiento led the riots and rapidly became the city's commander-in-chief. Until then the event could have been considered a typical case of political opposition and rebellion against the state due to a fiscal rebellion. The crown could not abide by such an affront to its authority, and Álvaro de Luna sent his troops to Toledo to snuff out the rebellion.

The conflict, however, had a specific twist. In order to shield himself from public opinion and justify his conduct, Pero Sarmiento used the convert issue to his advantage. Jews, especially the converts among them, were accused of being responsible for the problems at hand. They were accused of abusing their positions of great influence in local administration since the beginning of the century, exploiting the misery of the people, and enriching themselves at their expense.

As on other such occasions, street preacher-prophets like the so-called Bachelor Marquitos, who claimed to be directly inspired by the Holy Spirit, contributed to inciting the resistance and added religious conflict to motivate the rebellion. He argued that Jews had always been the enemies of the people and of Spain, that Jews committed treason in handing over the peninsula to the Moors in the eighth century, and that the converts, despite their baptisms, were of the same stock. These declarations and insinuations, demagogic in character, excited people even more and justified the excessive violence and pillaging committed mainly against converts. Sarmiento played an active role and managed to sack an enormous fortune for himself.[27]

As the veritable master of the city for several months, on June 5, 1449, Sarmiento promulgated a famous edict, the *Sentencia Estatuto,* known as the first blood-cleansing statute in the history of Spain. His order thus excluded converts from all public functions (council governments and public office as well as acting as notaries). Thus the revolt of 1449 in Toledo manifested three characteristics in its chronological development. First, it began as a popular insurrection motivated by a fiscal issue and, as such, a social issue. Second, it continued as a political rebellion against Álvaro de Luna's government. Third, then and only then, in an attempt to justify it ideologically, it was used as anti-convert propaganda and resulted in the promulgation of a discriminatory legal sentence.

Toledo only returned to a more normal existence at the beginning of the year 1450. Sarmiento's edict was revoked. The rebellion was strictly limited to that city and Ciudad Real and did not spread to the rest of the kingdom. Apparently nothing happened in other areas such as Burgos, Segovia, and Andalusia, where there were many converts. Events in Toledo did, however, have widespread repercussions. It was the first time the issue of converts—not that of Jews—was used as an instrument in political action and transformed into a matter of public order. Moreover, the discriminatory sentence statute introduced inflamed polemics over the converts' situation in Spanish Christian society.[28]

The official reaction of the Church was immediate and blunt. A papal bull, *Humani generis inimicus* (Pope Nicholas V, September 24, 1449), condemned Sarmiento's edict and annulled all its dispositions as contrary to the unity of the Christian people. All Christians, whatever their date of baptism, were to be considered brothers in Christ and have equal right to obtain ecclesiastical or civil offices and positions.[29] The former prior of the Dominican convent of San Marcos de Toledo, Cardinal Juan de Torquemada, intervened in much the same spirit. His *Tractatus contra Madianistas et Ismaelitas,* written in Rome in 1450, wholeheartedly attacked the validity of Sarmiento's statute. There was to be no discrimination made between old and new Christians with regard to holding public office. Lope de Barrientos, the bishop of Cuenca, was of the same opinion (*Contra algunos cizañadores*), stating that it was true heresy to receive someone into the faith and baptize him only to deny him access to public office afterward. Indeed, Sarmiento's statute received an immediate and clear-cut condemnation, but the issue had not been definitively settled.

The political discord unleashed during the second half of the reign of Enrique IV, especially as of 1462 when the crisis dissolved into civil war, reactivated hostility against Jews and converts. The power struggle had to be settled to determine who held the greatest influence in the highest spheres, that is, would or would not the crown be subjected to the tutelage of a band of nobles. The attacks against converts were not substantially different from those directed at the same time against the educated class. Both groups had benefited from a rise in social status and offered their experience and talents to serve the crown. Even more, it was a reaction against the collective promotion of converts. The resentment reached such a degree that hatred of converts became even stronger than hatred of Jews.

For Enrique IV's adversaries the Jewish and convert problem was nothing more than a subject for demagogical propaganda in order to strangle royal power and gain backing from the exploited masses. Thus, in 1461 a Franciscan, Brother Hernando de la Plaza, was heard preaching in Madrid against false converts. His claim was that the crypto-Jewish converts had been circumcised. As proof, he said he had more than a hundred foreskins at his home! When required to display them upon his arrest by the king's forces the friar had to confess his lie. This rather grotesque incident attests to the level to which populist propaganda had sunk. Nobles did not stop at citing the king himself in a series of personal attacks. He was chided for wearing Moorish garb and criticized for enjoying the company of infidels as a friend and protector of Jews. The nobles demanded, among other things, that all court Jews be dismissed from their posts.

In this context anything could rekindle public rage and cause uprisings in major cities taking advantage of the general crisis situation and the lack of respect for authority. The farce of Avila (1464), the destitution of Enrique IV, and the proclamation of his son, infante Don Alfonso, brought state paralysis to its zenith. Each opposing side attempted to debilitate the others in any way possible. Jews, traditionally faithful to legitimate power, could only suffer the consequences of the conflict, as, in turn, did the converts.

The most serious incidents occurred in Andalusia. Carmona was sacked in 1464 when the governor, Beltrán de Pareja, attempted to vanquish the resistance of some nobles. He reverted to the convert issue, and rioters actually murdered some converts. In July 1465 the infante's partisans, led by Pedro de Stúñiga, ran through the streets of Seville screaming "Stúñiga! Stúñiga! In spite of Jewish whores!" The opposing side led by the Count of Niebla armed people who managed to keep the agitators at bay and prevented converts' houses from being sacked. "From here on," wrote the jurist Garcí Sánchez, "the converts maintained their honor, and no one dared say an unkind word against them."[30]

In simplistic fashion the power struggle was reduced to being one for or against converts, although that religious attitude camouflaged more transcendent ambitions. For three days in July 1467, infante Don Alonso's partisans fought Enrique IV's supporters in the streets of Toledo. Many converts' houses were burned, and some new Christians were hanged. The motive was apparently linked to the municipal cathedral chapter's (*cabildo catedralicio*) demand for a new special tax. On this occasion the converts had a defender in the Count of Cifuentes, Don Alonso de Léon, who was nevertheless unable to prevent robbery and murder. The rebels attempted to reestablish the 1449 statute and expand it to include discrimination against ecclesiastical benefits. Both on a local and national level the convert issue was transformed into a conflict despite the fact that nothing tangible justified it from a political or social viewpoint. It was an easy and demagogic way to obtain power, rightly or wrongly.

The final years of Enrique IV's reign were marked by a clear loss of prestige for the crown and intense class struggle offering many opportunities to designate Jews and converts as public enemies. Once again, blood was shed in several cities in Andalusia. In addition to this political discord, in 1473 the Guadalquivir Valley suffered economic hardship due to bad harvests, price hikes, food shortages, and epidemics.

All this laid the ground for anti-Jewish propaganda. Once again the theme of the Hebrew exploiter as cause and beneficiary of popular misery was brandished. The most cruel and inhumane events occurred in Córdoba. The apparent cause was that the Lord of Aguilar, Alfonso Fernández de Córdoba, the most influential man in town, was considered to be a friend and protector of converts. His opponents used this situation to promote a riot on March 17, 1473, that was immediately turned against converts. Diego de Valera wrote, "The new Christians of that city were very rich and had been known to buy positions they used in such a haughty manner that the old Christians could no longer stand it."[31]

Hatred and social rejection as motivations were in the foreground. In reality, what was occurring was a class struggle, the poor pitted against the rich, but certain wealthy people opportunistically used the convert issue to reinforce their own influence and domination. All the tumultuous disturbances during the years from 1449 to 1474 coincided with serious subsistence crises. Thus the social aspect of the problem was its main feature; the anti-Jewish or anti-convert aspect is secondary and always appears as ideological justification for actions already taken.

Due to these revolts reminiscent of what occurred after 1391, many Andalusian converts emigrated to Flanders or Italy.[32] Many more sought refuge on land under seignorial jurisdiction, whether in Gibraltar, fiefdom of the Duke of Medina Sidonia, or in Baena, property of the Count of Cabra. The protection of certain magnates must also be taken into account in evaluating the precise role of the aristocracy in establishing the Inquisition and expelling the Jews.

In the meantime the dynastic contest reached its conclusion. Many in the kingdom—including members of the nobility—were deeply worried by the chaos and anarchy and subsequent excesses of violence. These nobles placed their hopes in Princess Isabel, Enrique IV's sister. Isabel was seen as the best choice to reestablish the prestige and authority of the crown and thereby restore public order in Castile. Those opposed to this plan, such as Juan Pacheco, defended the ascension of Doña Juana, the *"Beltraneja,"* who—they believed—would allow them to continue occupying dominant positions and gaining fortune at the expense of the royal patrimony. Segovia and its castle, where the royal treasure was kept, were of primary importance for the outcome of events. Don Juan Pacheco tried to make himself the master of Segovia in 1472 and 1473 and in his attempt reverted to the typical arguments of his clan, using a purge of converts as a cover to satisfy his ambitions. He was resolutely opposed by the governor, Andrés de Cabrera, a convert who had long been convinced that Princess Isabel alone would be capable of ending the civil war and inaugurating an era of prosperity with strong and well-respected royal power. Another Segovian, the eastern Jew Abraham Seneor, an important tax collector, also felt that Isabel was the answer. So indeed it came to pass that in December of 1474 the young princess emerged from her castle two days after the death of her brother Enrique IV and proclaimed herself queen and rightful heir to Castile.

～ 4
Jews and Converts in the Catholic Monarchs' Spain
(1474–92)

With the crowning of Queen Isabel in Castile at the end of 1474 in conjunction with the coronation of her husband, Fernando, in Aragon in 1479 Spain began its extraordinary rise to power. It would be better to avoid an excessively individualistic interpretation of events; the new monarchs produced no miracles. They came to the throne in a country full of potential, especially in Castile where there was great dynamism and vitality. Among other positive factors, Spain was benefiting from steady population growth and a resurgent economy, mainly in wheat farming, which provided consistent income and led to the significant development of foreign trade. This was not a situation the monarchs created; it already existed. It was, however, one obfuscated by political struggles and the ambitions of nobles avid for wealth and power.

In short, the nation needed peace and order to be able to prosper, and the monarchs enabled Spain to take advantage of its opportunities. They were able to reestablish the prestige of the crown, positioning it above the divisive factions. Royal authority was reaffirmed such that no group, whether the nobility, municipal powers, popular courts, or Church, could act against it. The monarchs founded several institutions, an administration and a form of government that in many ways had a clearly modern character, most of which was later maintained by the House of Austria.

Of course, these improvements were the result of a long process. The king and queen first had to beat the opposition through a war of succession and vanquish those nostalgic for the previous reign. Beyond a civil struggle, the conflict also involved the invasion of foreign troops on Spanish territory. Thus we consider that the reorganization of the state was basically created in the Courts of Toledo (1480).

It is important to insist once again on an often-repeated observation: For Jews, there was no better guarantee of safety than a strong and respected state power capable of imposing authority throughout the territory and preventing disorder. In this regard the change in policy became rapidly patent; the monarchs were intent on preventing any and all violence. After a few incidents in Trujillo, Isabel signed a charter on July 7, 1477, placing the aljama under her royal protection in order to enforce a ban against any oppression or humiliation of Jews:

> I order each and every one of you that from now on no gentlemen or squires or other persons nor any people from this city or outside of it compel or oblige these aforementioned Jews. . . . to clean his stables or wash his water jars . . . or threaten them or send ruffians, strumpets or people to their houses against their wishes.[1]

Previously, the basic principle defining the position of the crown with regard to Jews was "all Jews in my kingdom are mine and under my protection and guardianship and it is my responsibility to protect them and give them asylum and maintain justice." That position was reaffirmed on September 6 in Seville:

> By this charter I posit and receive under my guardianship, protection and royal defense the aforementioned Jews from the aforementioned *aljamas* and I insure each one of them and their families and possessions against any and all people whoever they are and I command and order that [these people] not harm, kill or injure them or let them be harmed, killed or injured.[2]

On August 12, 1490, two years before the expulsion decree, that position was reiterated in a decree intended for the Bilbao council: "According to canon law and according to the laws of our kingdoms, the Jews are tolerated and accommodated, and We hereby order that they be tolerated and permitted to live in our kingdoms as Our subjects and vassals."[3]

Most of the documents published by Luis Suárez Fernández on the Catholic monarchs' Jewish policy between 1474 and 1492 concern protests against abuses and ill-treatment of Jews by towns and individuals with concurrent requests for the strict application of existing policies to protect them. The desired result was not always forthcoming. There were cases in which towns returned to abusing Jews and mocked the monarchs' authority.[4] The general tendency, however, was always the same: asylum for and protection of Jews against all violence, humiliation, and abuse. That is the main reason the monarchs were quickly criticized for showing extreme favor to Jews. Nicholas de

Popielovo, who visited Spain in 1484, said, "Their subjects in Catalonia and Aragon speak of it publicly and I heard it said by many in Spain that the queen is the protector of the Jews and herself the daughter of a Jewess." In 1487 the same Castilian Jews were joined by the Hebrew communities of Rome and Lombardy in praising the Catholic monarchs for their justice and charity.[5] Luis Suárez Fernández is certainly not far from the truth when he writes that had Fernando and Isabel died in 1491 their names would have gone down in Jewish history with a completely different connotation.[6]

Catholic monarchs attempted to end bloody attacks against Jews and converts to prevent incidents similar to those that occurred during past reigns.[7] They were not, however, able to halt a series of rumors, prejudices, and insinuating and irrational accusations spread and fed by irresponsible preachers as well as various writings that together made the popular phobia of Jews close to racism. Jews were still and all considered collectively as a hostile, dangerous, and repugnant group of people whose members were called dirty pigs (*Marranos*).[8] Proverbs were a good source of the more usual anti-Jewish stereotypes and often characterized Jews as having long noses, sunken eyes, and dirty teeth, not unlike the image represented in more contemporary iconography. These characterizations also tended to convey a contradictory moral and psychological portrait. Jews were fearful and cowardly yet also arrogant.[9]

Tricky and untrustworthy, rancorous and vengeful, Jews were also considered intelligent and capable, especially in business matters. From this point on the theme of usury was often on the list as was the typical accusation that Jews were Christ-murderers. Moreover, the stereotypical Jew was seen as having a penchant for all kinds of vice, including sodomy.[10] The *Coplas del provincial* composed between 1465 and 1474 was a violent allegation in octosyllabic verse against Enrique IV and Spanish nobility. In crude terms the text attacked well-known converts such as Diego Arias Dávila, the king's chief accountant.[11] In addition, the phobia against Jews included repeated accusations of various sacrileges (profaning the host and scalding in freezing water) and ritual crimes.[12] The most representative example was the case of Niño de la Guardia just before the expulsion of 1492.

Priests of the mendicant orders were intent on communicating irrational fears to the Old Christian masses. For example, there was the Dominican in Segovia in 1485 who called Christian believers' attention to the danger of eating food prepared or even touched by Jews. There were mayors who prohibited Jews from baking bread in public ovens so as not to contaminate Christians' bread. Some councils complained of Jewish disloyalty toward Christians because the former worked on Sundays or made noise in their workshops while the latter were in church. The festivities of the Holy Week, with the traditional remembrance of Judas's treachery toward Jesus Christ and the death of Jesus, constituted a special occasion for insults, vexations, and humiliating discrimination. In Vitoria in 1488 the Jews representing the synagogue had to walk through a double line of men and women who called them dogs, spat in their faces, and hit them as they passed.

Luis Suárez Fernández, who has documented most of these insulting incidents, concludes confidently that the sorry state of affairs contributed to creating pessimism, fear, and resignation among Jews. Despite official royal protection this hateful atmosphere foreshadowed what appeared inevitable. As has occurred several times in history, Jews compensated for the tense situation by placing their hopes in Messianic movements. The Messiah was coming, the prophet would return. Documents found in Andalusia that date from just before the expulsion edict mention the Antichrist appearing in Seville.

How many Jews were in Spain at the beginning of the reign of the Catholic monarchs? The conversions of the fifteenth century had considerably reduced their numbers. Before the expulsion there were probably fewer than two hundred thousand Jews, of which 150 thousand were settled in Castilian territory and fifty thousand in the Kingdom of Aragon. All in all, Jews represented fewer than 2 percent of the total population of the double monarchy. These figures from Baer tend to exaggerate the numbers for Castile and are definitely excessive for the Kingdom of Aragon. More recent figures estimate that no more than twenty thousand Jews were in Aragon. Ladero's calculations, extrapolated from the 1480 tax ledger called *servicio y medio servicio* (service and mid-service, a special tax only Jews paid), reveal that the Jewish population was thinly dispersed throughout Castilian territory. More than four hundred localities had Jewish populations grouped into some two hundred aljamas.[13]

The distribution of taxpayers allows us to trace a geographic map of Castilian Judaism at the end of the fifteenth century. The great aljamas of the fourteenth century—in Seville, Toledo, and Burgos—had either disappeared or were no longer thriving. In the fifteenth century small populations of Jews lived outside the largest cities. The most important Jewish communities were then located in Segovia, Toledo,[14] Trujillo, Guadalajara, Ocaña, Almazán, Soria, Avila,[15] Valladolid, and Murcia, with more than three hundred families in each. The highest density was located in northern Castile, especially in the bishopric of Palencia, which accounted for 14 percent of the total Jewish population of Kingdom of Castile. Immediately following in terms of Jewish population was the archbishopric of Toledo with 13.46 percent. Extremadura and Andalusia together accounted for fewer than 12 percent of the Jewish population despite the extensive area, and the same was true for the bishoprics of León and Astorga. There were expanses of land, for example, Asturias, had no Jews to speak of. Galicia had only two aljamas, Orense and La Coruña. The Basque country also had two as did Valmaseda and especially Vitoria, the most populous Jewish community in the northern plateau of Castile, which harbored more Jews than the much larger town of Burgos.

Andrés Bernáldez, priest of Los Palacios, left a well-known portrayal of Castilian Jews immediately preceding their expulsion from Spain:

> These Jews from Castile lived in the best cities, villas and places on the best tracts of lands. They were all merchants, salesmen, tax or rent collectors, cloth-shearers, tailors, shoemakers, tanners, curriers, weavers, grocers, peddlers, silk-mercers, silversmiths (jewelers), and the like. . . . Not one of them worked the land or was a carpenter or mason, but they all sought easy jobs and ways of earning a lot of money without working too hard.

Bernáldez was confusing Jews and converts, which is interesting in and of itself. Like many of his contemporaries he made no true distinction between the two groups.

A historian, however, should not commit the same error. With the facts we have now it is possible to rectify and correct this picture, which appears inexact in any light and clearly more in line with the author's prejudices than with historical reality. Not all Jews lived in cities, large or small; many lived in rural villages and worked in agriculture. It is probable that the killings of 1391 and subsequent violent attacks had motivated Jews to live in the country or in small-town areas thought to be less exposed than urban zones to disruptive uprisings. There is little information about Jews who raised cattle and owned vineyards. In cities such as Buitrago or Hita many owned fields, pastures, and vineyards.[16] In Toledo most Jews farmed. In Segovia as of 1469, public records attest to the acquisition of land and vineyards by Abraham Seneor in places such as Pinilla, Ambroz, and Pinillos.[17] There was indeed a preference for acquiring livestock, vineyards, and on occasion, gold and silver, that is, easily transportable or convertible wealth in the event of compromising social or political events. Those preferences, however, were not uniquely characteristic of Jews but also true of medieval Castilian society on the whole as Father Corominas mentioned many years ago.[18]

Similarly, an extremely disproportionate number of Jews did not work as craftsmen. Américo Castro's thesis on the supposed technical incapacity of Castilians remains unproven. Naturally, many Jews worked as craftsmen or in trades, most in a modest manner, although some exercised their talents in a more sumptuous fashion, as in Aragon. Yet Jews worked alongside Christians who performed the same trades and were much more numerous than they in these occupations. This is one of the most repeated and discussed themes that present-day archival research is working to clarify about Jews of the period. They did specialize in certain occupations such as medicine, but many fewer than originally believed. There was no Jewish monopoly in commerce, for example, and by the reign of the Catholic monarchs the role of Jews had become peripheral, almost insignificant, in international trade. For the most part, converts held on to these kinds of businesses. The large majority of Jews were simple shopkeepers and merchants.

As for the controversial theme of Jews as money handlers, it is undeniably true that there were moneylenders among them, and some charged very high rates of interest. Jewish usury was a convenient diversion to hide certain financial realities that no one wanted to disclose. The odd thing is that, on occasion, we have examples of individual members of the clergy defending Jews to help them recover their debts. On a relatively frequent basis Jews served as figureheads for ecclesiastical institutions involved in this type of business. In order to get rid of complaints of usury dating from before 1476, in 1484 some Jews offered a special donation of close to 2 million *maravedís* in exchange for general amnesty. The monarchs accepted the deal because they had already fixed the maximum rate of interest at 30 percent in the Courts of Madrigal (1476). Although it seems incredible, a 30 percent interest must have seemed reasonable to borrowers at the time. The theme of usury remained one of the most frequently used arguments against Jews in spite of the fact that the number of Jewish moneylenders had decreased and more and more Christians practiced the profession.

Since the reign of Enrique II it had become rare for Jews to be named royal treasurers, tax collectors, or accountants. There were many more who were royal, ecclesiastical, or seignorial rent collectors, but even in that area significant changes had occurred in the first half of the fifteenth century. Ladero, to whom we owe a very fine investigation of the question, arrived at the same conclusion, that between 1439 and 1469 only seventy-two of some five hundred rent collectors listed were Jews—approximately 15 percent. Those Jewish rent collectors handled no more than a fourth of the total collections, among them the tithes from Castile, the service tax, and cattle tolls from the salt mines of Atienza. The other contributions or taxes were handled by converts or old Christians, although at times Jews were known to intervene as assistant collectors, for example, in the collection of rents for the Cathedral of Leon.[19] The situation remained largely unchanged during the reign of the Catholic monarchs, and by 1480 only a few hundred Jews were still employed in these professions.

At court things were different, at least in Castile. In the Kingdom of Aragon, Jews' influence had significantly decreased. By the reigns of Alfonso V and Juan II (1458–79) Jews were no longer exercising key administrative or financial functions, and nothing substantially new occurred with Fernando the Catholic given that Aragonese Judaism had already faded from its past glory, but the same was not true of the Court of Castile. There the key figure was Abraham Seneor, who as of 1475 was rapidly promoted from his post as major director (*alguacil mayor*) of the aljama of Segovia, a position he had occupied since 1470. By the following year he had advanced to the position of major tax collector, and in 1488 he became the major treasurer of the Holy Brotherhood, a highly prominent office given the role monarchs assigned it in financing the war of Granada. Thus enormous quantities of taxes were collected for the Brotherhood, whose own troops occupied the battlefield. From the beginning of the reign Abraham Seneor appeared as one of the monarchs' most efficient collaborators and one to whom the highest financial responsibilities were entrusted. Another Jew who advanced at the time was Yosef Abravanel. In 1488 he was the general collector for the party of Plasencia and obtained the role of primary collector of the service tax and cattle toll, one of the most guaranteed taxes and the main revenue for the Kingdom of Castile.

Despite all this documented evidence one should not draw unreasonable conclusions such as those we have become accustomed to seeing in historiography that tends to be full of approximations and preconceived ideas on the subject. Werner Sombart at the beginning of this century, and more recently Américo Castro and Claudio Sánchez-Albornoz, surprisingly in agreement on this point, have presented Jews as the main drivers of the economy and thus the main movers of capitalism and progress in Spain. In their view, the expulsion of Jews provoked widespread decadence in the country, which was later incapable of substituting Christian bankers and entrepreneurs for Jews.

Nothing, however, supports this contention in the documentation researchers have investigated in the national and regional archives. The Jews' role has been greatly exaggerated not only in terms of tax collection and the organization of the royal treasury but also with regard to economic life in general. At the end of the fifteenth century in Spain their role was, in fact, a minor one. The truth is that the crown was able to do without Jews, whether in organizing its bureaucratic apparatus or managing the public treasury and royal properties. In many cases converts took over these roles; in others, old Christians were in charge. Hatred for Jews rose to its zenith at precisely the time the number of those involved in these businesses had been considerably reduced.

We therefore have to refute this assertion spread by propaganda at the time and later revived and amplified by essayists and historians with few archival sources. We do not see an immensely rich and influential Jewish community managing the essential resources of the nation—including the royal treasury, taxes, and large-scale commerce—and exploiting old Christians. In reality, at the time of their expulsion Spanish Jews did not form a socially homogeneous group. As in Christian society there were classes within the group, including a small minority of very wealthy men in high positions and a large majority of "little people," farmers, artisans, and shopkeepers. Between the two, as in the rest of society, there were slight grudges and disagreements, including hatred and exploitation of the weak by the powerful.[20] All had a common characteristic: They partook in the same beliefs and practiced the same faith. That faith was what made Jews in Spain a separate community with a certain degree of autonomy within the monarchy.

This is the key point for understanding the situation of Jews in Spain and allows a better grasp of the motives for their expulsion. Because Jews were tolerated within the Christian community and authorized to practice a religion different from the official one, they were not treated as individuals involved in a merely private matter but rather as a collective body. Jews were subjects and vassals of the crown, as Queen Isabel often reiterated. As such, when they benefited from rents of more than 30,000 maravedís annually they had the obligation, like Christians in the same condition, to keep a horse and arm themselves to fight in war although they served in the military separate from Christians.[21] They were subjects of the crown not as particular individuals but as members of a community that had a legal, accepted, and recognized existence through the state.

Within that community Jews were more or less freely organized. Each aljama functioned as an autonomous municipal council. They had leaders, the council of elders, elected by casting lots, and they handled matters related to internal government and dictated rules and their enforcement. They also collected the necessary funds for maintaining a collective life, religious activities, and the upkeep of synagogues; Talmudic teaching; and everything related to religious ritual, including burials and cemeteries.[22] Within aljamas there were also brotherhoods similar to Christian fraternities, whose role it was to assist the poor and infirm. Life developed in accordance with the moral and juridical rules of Judaism. There were special judges who heard complaints between Jews in civil matters but since the 1476 decision made by the Courts of Madrigal not in criminal matters. In line with their general politics of removing penal jurisdiction from all particular corporations, the Catholic monarchs had abolished the aljamas' privilege of judging penal cases.[23]

Jews had a specific fiscal regime. From 1437 on they no longer contributed to municipal taxes because they formed a separate community. The Catholic monarchs confirmed this measure in 1477 in spite of protests by certain councils.[24] Jews paid many more taxes than Christians yet their contributions were made directly through the "servicio y medio servicio" instituted during the fifteenth century. To collect this contribution, the crown used the apparatus created by Abraham Benveniste and held a few periodic assemblies where representatives of aljamas met with royal officials. These assemblies fixed the amount each aljama had to pay, according to its importance, in order to reach the total sum required by the crown. Each aljama thus divided the payment among its members according to the ability of each family to pay.

These popular assemblies—which evolved into something like the parliament—allowed the Hebrew community to address matters of collective interest. Attendants at an assembly of this type in 1484 in Maqueda discussed in particular the burning question of usury and the manner in which to comply with the laws decreed in 1476 and 1480. The structure was completed by the figure of the *rab mayor* (a person named by the sovereign as his intermediary and spokesperson with the Jewish community). Abraham Benveniste occupied the position during the reign of Juan II, when Castilian Judaism was rebuilt after the crisis years from 1391 to 1415. The Catholic monarchs appointed Abraham Seneor, who enjoyed their total confidence.

Thus Jews formed an autonomous and separate community within society. They did not enjoy full civil rights. They were indeed excluded from several offices, including any position in which they would have authority over Christians. They bore a disproportionately large tax burden, the price for their autonomy. Within those limits, however, they organized their lives as they wished in accordance with their religious and cultural habits. As a legally existing entity, the aljama participated in various events with an official character. It is worth citing Hernando de Pulgar's chronicle about the celebration made when Alonso de Burgos became bishop of Palencia in 1486. Palencia was an episcopal domain, so the aljama was represented in the official ceremony.[25] Pulgar states:

> There were great festivities where particularly the Moors and Jews of the city, who were their vassals, rejoiced; the Moors dancing various dances and inventions and the Jews singing things of their law in procession, followed by a rabbi who carried a roll of parchment in his hands, covered with an embroidered cloth which they said was the Torah; and the bishop arrived and made a reverence according to the law of God, because he said that it was the Holy Scripture of the Old Testament, and with authority, he took it in his hands and then threw it backwards, onto his shoulders, to signify that it was past by, and from behind, he passed it along to the rabbi. This dignified ceremony should be remembered, for it was the last time [such an event] was celebrated, because afterwards, a few years later, they all became Christians.

—*Jews and Converts (1474–1492)*

Rather than a state within the state, Jews formed a microsociety and lived alongside the dominant Christian society with authority over members as delegated by the crown. This situation, which appears to be particular to Spain, created two main problems. First, as subjects and vassals of the crown Jews had no guarantees for their futures. At any time the monarchy could decide to limit the authority of aljamas or demand new and more burdensome taxes. Second, and most important, during these last years of the Middle Ages a great philosophical question was posed concerning the modern character of government. Was it possible for autonomous and separate communities to coexist given the hegemony required by the modern state power? That was the crux of the matter.

During the reign of the Catholic monarchs many within the Church, and a good part of the masses in particular, continued to consider Jews as enemies of their faith and a menace to Christian society as a whole. It is true, however, that this hatred had been largely displaced toward new Christians or converts, mainly against Jews baptized at the end of the fourteenth and the beginning of the fifteenth century. Converts constituted a significant minority of some 250 to three hundred thousand men and women who were spread throughout Spain but nevertheless exhibited some salient characteristics in common.

It is not surprising to note that the geographic and sociological map of convert populations appears as the negative of that of Jews. In areas where persecutions were the most severe and most frequent, Jews tended to convert in greater numbers. Where there were fewer incidents Jews continued to outnumber converts. In Andalusia, for example, the concentration of new Christians was impressive. Almost half of these converts lived in large cities (Seville, Ecija, and Jerez) and a very few on royal rural land. The rest established themselves in domains under the protection of individual nobles and magnates (the dukes of Medina Sidonia, Arcos, and Medinaceli and the lords of Moguer, Palos, Gibraléon, and Ayamonte). Almost all converts, in Andalusia as in the rest of Spain, were involved in artisanry, commerce, services, administrative or financial administration, and public office. Very few were farmers. Converts indeed resembled what Bernáldez said of Jews: "none of them touched the soil [broke the earth]." Bernáldez was a major exponent for an entire sector of public opinion that lumped Jews and converts together to criticize them with a special brand of racism. Julio Caro Baroja clearly described this typology:

> The convert is a man from the city, from the street, from the marketplace. Among the genealogies belonging to this cast, there are last names that recall this attribute: *Ciudad* [city], *La Calle* or *De la Calle* [from the street], the *Mercado* [market], the name *Franco* [Frank, Free] and their abundant Italian and Portuguese equivalents. The convert is, in most cases, a bourgeois in the vague sense that word is given today, a bourgeois and often a nouveau riche.[26]

The information we have on converts in Segovia, Burgos, Toledo, Barcelona, Valencia, and Palma confirms this characterization.[27]

According to Julio Caro Baroja, for the most part converts behaved like the nouveaux riche. That observation merits comment in light of what Bernáldez has written: "They had a presumption of arrogance." It was not that converts thought they were free to do as they pleased but rather that they had the impression they were better endowed and had an advantage over old Christians, which was true from a legal point of view. In essence, they could hold offices and receive privileges previously denied them and which continued to be denied to Jews. As we have seen, many converts entered into municipal councils and the clergy. They sometimes occupied positions that gave them authority and jurisdiction over old Christians. In addition, they exercised professions—in commerce and tax collection—that made them the target of resentment in times of crisis (bad harvests, austerity, and famines). Converts were accused of stockpiling wheat and flour to sell it to the poor at inflated prices and being overly harsh in demanding taxes during difficult times.

Old Christians viewed converts as they had the Jews before them, as hucksters and exploiters who without pity or consideration selfishly took advantage of others' misery. Detested as exploiters, the reaction against Jews was the result of a social situation (class hatred) augmented by ideological justifications. It was said that Jews, now disguised as Christians, mistreated Christian people. During periods of temporary crises the opposition of poor versus rich was transformed into a conflict between converts and/or old Jews versus old Christians. There is no way to underestimate the importance of these ideological aspects. People were convinced that converts were hypocrites who had been baptized to better exploit Christians while continuing to be Jews.

For the masses, all converts were false Christians. A group of historians has evaluated this accusation, which was the basis for establishing the Inquisition, and labeled it a pretext, nothing more than an ideological mask dissimulating class struggle. Converts were Catholics, nothing more, nothing less. If they had been accused of being hypocrites it was only to eliminate them as a social class occupying positions of power that threatened traditional groups.

Today, however, we can no longer deny the existence of peninsular crypto-Judaism. It would be useful to evaluate the extent and significance of this phenomenon. There is no doubt that many conversions were not sincere. Because conversions were overwhelmingly inspired by terror and the threat of persecution, once the bloodshed was over perhaps it was true that many converts regretted their decision. In late medieval society, however, it was impossible to change one's mind about such things. Once baptized, converts and their descendants became Christians forever. There was a serious contradiction in

Catholic doctrine as it was taught at the time. On one hand, there was the principle that faith is an act of free will and no one can force anyone else to embrace Christianity. This is the principle that Thomas Aquinas constantly defended and the one recalled in the sixteenth century with respect to the indigenous populations of the Americas. In order to be valid, conversion had to be sincere.[28] On the other hand, conversion to Christianity was considered irreversible, even if it was not voluntary. Anyone who was baptized and subsequently changed religions was therefore a heretic and became subject to the most severe punishments, including death. In medieval Christianity, religion was a matter of individual belief as well as a social and collective institution. One who might drift from faith and dogma as defined by the church would be guilty of not just an individual sin but of threatening the cohesion of the social body whose foundation was precisely this faith.[29] For that reason a Catholic who departed from the faith was punished as not just a sinner but rather as a public enemy and "traitor to the Republic."[30]

Under these conditions, assuming they wanted to do so, new Christians who converted between 1391 and 1415 could not change their minds. On the contrary, if they attempted such a move they would expose themselves to an even greater danger: Society would condemn them to death. The only solution was to continue being Catholic, at least in public, and to practice Judaism at home in secret if they had any scruples about Catholicism. Thus, there were indeed those who led a double life. Although they were Christian in appearance and as such followed the precepts of the Church (attending mass and receiving the sacraments), they were really Jews who took great precaution to avoid calling attention to themselves when observing certain rites of the law of Moses (circumcision, the Sabbath, prayers, and fasting).

This situation is described by an inquisitor in a tract published in 1488 and entitled the *Libro del Alborayque*. False converts appeared to Alborayque like Mohammed's beast of burden that was neither horse nor mule. Pulgar related some astonishing cases: "In certain houses, the husband practiced specific Jewish rites while the wife continued to be a good Christian or the daughter practiced the Christian religion while the son held Jewish opinions. And [thus] within a single household, there was a diversity of beliefs, even hidden from one another." At the beginning of the sixteenth century, Leonor, one of the daughters of a convert named Juan de Lucena, expressed the same idea in a graphic manner to her sister in a letter dated August 12, 1510, describing her family as "one who didn't know day from night."[31]

Although there is no doubt about some converts' crypto-Judaism in the fifteenth century and that contemporaries were well aware of its existence, until the establishment of the Inquisition such practices went unpunished.

Clearly, it was not because practicing Judaism in secret was tolerated or a matter of indifference.[32] Rather, it was because there had been no appropriate legal instrument available to deal with this type of crime. With the creation of the tribunal of the Inquisition authorities obtained an adequate instrument that provided the means to investigate and punish these offenses.

The edict of faith evolved into a minute inventory of practices and affirmations considered as Jewish (celebrating the Sabbath, eating meat on fast days, reciting Hebrew prayers, and observing Passover and other Jewish holidays), including a wide reference to funerary rituals.[33] All this was accompanied by a call to denounce and a threat to excommunicate those who continued to observe any of these Jewish practices.[34] In investigating incidents, inquisitors would sometimes go back some eighty years to recapitulate events, that is, to the date of the first massive conversions. It was discovered that before the strict segregation of the 1480s many converts would join Jewish friends in celebrating various holidays, attending synagogue, listening to sermons, and discussing matters of faith. They would also observe the (Saturday) Sabbath and other holidays and recite Hebrew prayers.

The inquisitorial trials were replete with specific cases. For example, at the death of the governor (*regidor*) Fernando de la Torre, a convert, Hebrew liturgy was found in his home in Toledo along with receipts for his participation in rabbinical charities.[35] On May 7, 1487, a canonist was burned who "wore a Hebrew cross in his shirt to the right of the host." He confessed under torture that when he celebrated mass, instead of pronouncing the consecration he would say, "Hurry and show yourself to the people!"[36] Several Geronimo friars of Guadalupe were burned for practicing Judaism in 1485. In 1491 a posthumous trial was opened against Fernán Sánchez de Villanueva, a convert from Quintanar de la Orden. His son, Pero de Villanueva, testified as remembering having seen his father read Hebrew prayerbooks. Villanueva noted that on Saturdays his father would stay in bed and that he only ate meat when he was sure that it came from a Jewish butcher; that he never ate ham or fish with scales.[37] In Valencia in January 1500 a secret synagogue was discovered in Luis Vives's uncle's home. It would be tedious to continue enumerating facts such as these to demonstrate the reality of Spanish crypto-Judaism at the end of the fifteenth century and even afterward.[38]

Several converts condemned by the Inquisition professed the Jewish faith and at the last minute refused to reconcile with Christianity. That attitude deserves respect because they were threatened with a most horrible death, being burned alive, whereas the fate of those who recognized their errors and reconciled with Christianity at the last minute was to be hanged before being delivered into the flames. All these people died as martyrs.

The reality of crypto-Judaism is now a rigorously documented fact that even historians who are close followers of Judaism admit without reservations.[39] One can believe whatever one wants of the Inquisition. It was a barbaric institution that acted harshly against those who refused to share official beliefs or those who wanted to distance themselves from them. Nevertheless, the Inquisition did not create a false problem. It did not itself invent offenders and persecute sincere Christian converts only to have a reason to burn them or despoil them.[40]

Such acts in a predominantly Christian society impregnated with religious sentiments could only provoke scandal and reprobation. Of course, not all converts were involved in crypto-Judaism. In reality, things were much more complicated. First, there were sincere converts who acted as good Christians. It is difficult to evaluate their numerical importance although they probably constituted the majority. Moreover, the Inquisition trials, which began in 1480 and were characterized by terrible harshness and repressive measures, did not address the entire Jewish convert population. It is reasonable to estimate that approximately half the convert population, a total of some 250 to three hundred thousand people, escaped all forms of persecution. Many false converts avoided being caught by the Inquisition, and an undeniable portion of converts lived and believed as sincere Christians. In addition, it is logical to assume that assimilation had progressed by the second or third generation. Furthermore, two sets of practices should be clear among sincere converts, the specifically religious one and the sociocultural one. In their fanaticism, various detractors of converts confused faith and custom.[41] When Bernáldez relates that some converts washed infants after baptism, the insinuation was that the converts were attempting to erase the baptismal marks. It is likely, however, that they were simply washing the baby as tradition would have it, nothing more.[42]

The implications of this observation can be extended to a great number of specific cases cited as signs of Jewish practices in the Inquisition's accusations. It allows us to understand Bernáldez's statement regarding the source of Jews' odor and the root of the expression *hediondos judíos* (repulsive, stinking Jews), which Bernáldez analyzed correctly but interpreted disparagingly:

> They never lost the habit of eating dishes prepared in the Jewish manner such as maize stew, savory dishes with refried onions and garlic in oil, and meat cooked with oil, used instead of bacon and pork meat fat; and [when one eats] meat cooked in oil, it makes one's breath smell very bad.

Bernáldez concluded, "The converts stunk like Jews . . . ; they smelled like Jews because of their food and because they were not baptized."

We can only ask what breath odor could possibly have to do with being baptized. Whether converts or Jews, these people were being upbraided not so much for their religion as for culinary habits that were less Jewish or Christian than Mediterranean in origin. For the old Christians from the northern plateaus of Castile where there were few olive trees the use of oil instead of lard must have seemed unusual and somehow repugnant. Jews and converts must have had the same feeling about northern cuisine. Now, of course, Spaniards have accustomed themselves to these southern cooking habits and the odors that go along with them. Although olive oil now figures as a typical ingredient in peninsular gastronomy, ancestors of the fifteenth century had very different customs. The same could be said of daily life—for example, changing clothing once a week on Saturdays.

It is absurd to regard culinary or other indifferent cultural practices as if they were religious or claim that they indicate one faith or another. Bernáldez knew that perfectly well: "Changing customs is like dying." It is easier to renounce religious beliefs or philosophical or political opinions than ancestral customs learned from childhood that have become part of one's personal day-to-day lifestyle. It is important to emphasize that these were precisely the accusations Bernáldez's contemporaries frequently made against converts.

Finally, a portion of converts, especially the most educated, were true religious skeptics. Although their numbers are difficult to estimate, these people preached religious indifference, including materialism *avant la lettre*. Baer and several other Jews have seen in those philosophical currents the consequences of controversies developed within Judaism emanating from several theories more or less related to Averroism. These theories struck at the bases of faith and morality. Among them was the idea that the soul is but a temporal form that ends existence with the death of its bearer. Thus, this philosophy could only give an allegorical interpretation of the Torah, when it did not make a complete mockery of it, by considering Aristotle's ideas as superior. Baer notes the case of Alfonso Fernández Semuel, who in his last will and testament ordered that a cross be placed at his feet, a Koran on his chest, and the Torah "up high and light" at his head in a clear demonstration of religious syncretism.[43] Baer also refers to the convert Alfonso de la Caballería, vice chancellor of Aragon, who kept reserved seats for himself and his family at the synagogue. Caballería is attributed with having stated, "In this world there is only birth and death; no other Paradise exists."[44] Ideas such as these were so manifestly current among some converts that we are led to refute Lucien Febvre's famous contention that atheism and materialism would have been inconceivable in Western Europe during the Renaissance because of the absence of the necessary conceptual equipment (*l'outillage mental*).[45]

The case of Spain radically disintegrates this thesis. Both in documents from the trials of the Inquisition and other sources from this era we discover frequent affirmations such as there is nothing but birth and death, and "in this world you will not see me fare poorly and in the next one you will not see me pain."[46] There has been much critical debate regarding the connections between Fernando de Rojas's work *La Celestina* and the convert problem. In my opinion this work bathes in the intellectual atmosphere of certain converts, including skepticism, indifference, and epicurianism. We can understand why some critics have noted the complete absence of all references of a religious character—either Catholic or Jewish—in the work.[47]

This philosophy of indifference continued to preoccupy the highest civil and ecclesiastical authorities. Not only was it a problem in confrontations between Jews, converts, and old Christians but also one of overall religious implications in the best sense of the word. The problem led to widespread controversy in intellectual circles. We have already mentioned the reaction to which Pero Sarmiento's statute on cleanliness of blood led when he attempted to impose it in Toledo in 1449. Basically, the reaction was a fundamental rejection of all discrimination based on a distinction between old and new Christians.

Later writings and treatises rehashed this theme, the complexity of which was gradually revealed. In *Lumen ad revelationem gentium* (1465) Brother Alonso de Oropesa voiced support for converts unjustly accused of "judaicizing" and suspected simply because they descended from Jews. Yet he also emphasized the Jews' responsibility not to be attracted to the faith of their former religion. Oropesa suggested a better solution: All Jews should convert to Christianity. In this way converts would be relieved of having to see relatives and friends continuing to live as Jews, which represented a constant temptation for them. Because the kingdom would be composed of Christians alone, all grudges would be ended.[48] It is true that Oropesa recommended peaceful conversions by means of persuasion and not force, yet it is interesting to observe how the bases for a definitive solution to the problem were already being contemplated and how that meant the total elimination of Judaism.

The *Fortalitium fidei* (1471) written by a Franciscan, Brother Alonso de Espina, was another important milestone. Confessor to Enrique IV, Espina was probably a convert himself although Baer doubts it. Espina attacks all types of infidels and heretics: Jews, Muslims, and false converts. Although he considers them all enemies of the Church, he is especially vehement in denouncing some converts' Averroist and materialist tendencies. Interestingly enough, Espina's study is one of the first known examples of religious sociology, given his approach and its subject is converts. He distinguishes three main categories of converts. First, there were sincere ones whose model would be the Santa María or Cartagena de Burgos families, people who became completely assimilated to Christianity. Next there were opportunists who received baptism in order to save their lives or keep their possessions and social position. Finally there were Jews who had been forced into conversion and had to be convinced. In addition to the elimination of Judaism, Alonso de Espina also recommended severe punishment for false Christians practicing crypto-Judaism.[49]

This describes the situation as it was in Spain when Fernando and Isabel came to power. Virtually unchanged since at least the beginning of the century, the situation was the result of the continuing existence of the Jewish community along with the presence of a strong minority of converts doubtful about the Catholic faith. Even taking into account the great religious fervor that in Spain as in the rest of Europe characterized late medieval society, I do not believe that the problem can be reduced to fanaticism alone. For the monarchs it was more a matter of public order. It was necessary to put an end to the antagonistic coexistence among Jews, converts, and old Christians. This was the reason for two complementary measures taken around 1480, one ensuring strict segregation of Jews apart from converts and the other creating a special tribunal for the punishment of Christian converts practicing Judaism.

In 1476 the Courts of Madrigal had already protested because the measures on discriminating against Jews, as stipulated by the Order of 1412 and regularly confirmed afterward, were not, in fact, being respected. Existing ordinances concerning Jews included one prohibiting them from wearing silk and the colors scarlet red, gold, and silver.[50] Others prohibited them holding specific offices and positions that would imply their authority over Christians, acquiring rural property valued at more than 30,000 maravedís, lending money at a usurious rate of interest, and employing Christian domestics. In addition, Jews were required to wear a red shield on their right shoulder as an ostentatious sign distinguishing them from non-Jews. In 1476 the monarchs limited themselves to reiterating the previous legislation. Once the War of Succession was over, however, the Courts of Toledo (1480) went much further in requiring an effective application of these laws. In order to do so, the most overwhelming measure used was a strict apartheid of Jews in separate gated neighborhoods they were allowed to leave only during the daytime to go to work. Although Jews had traditionally lived together in neighborhoods where their synagogues, butchers, stores, and workshops were located, these *juderías* (traditional Jewish neighborhoods) in no way constituted a separate world onto themselves.

Despite the laws there were Jews who lived outside the limits and mixed with the rest of the population. In addition, many Christians dwelt in Jewish neighborhoods for personal convenience, and when a decreasing Jewish population left many homes vacant even more Christians rented or bought property in these areas. No visible barrier existed to isolate the Jewish neighborhood from the rest of the city. Inhabitants came and went as they pleased. That all changed in 1480 with the establishment of veritable "ghettos," a term that refers to another place and time. The Catholic monarchs of Spain ordered that to avoid "confusion with and damage to our holy faith" all Jews within two years had to be concentrated within a single neighborhood encircled by walls, to which they would have to return every night, to prevent any and all communication with neighborhoods populated by Christians.

From this point on Christians who lived or stayed in the Jewish quarter had to leave it on a nightly basis. As opposed to earlier ordinances, the 1480 law was strictly enforced. Definite orders were expedited in this sense to the *corregidores* [magistrates], and special judges were named to handle the many complaints arising from its application. Clearly, segregation posed many practical problems. It was not always easy to mark off a border between neighborhoods, streets, and houses. In some areas the previously existing Jewish quarter was quite large and therefore had to be reduced for containment. Gates and walls were built, and the remainder of the property falling outside the ghetto's enclosure was sold off. Moreover, councils were not always willing to facilitate things for Jews and took advantage of the opportunity to sell houses and land at a premium, buying up Jewish-owned property at very low prices. The fluctuating negotiations, ensuing public works, and tense transactions lasted until the eve of the expulsion.

Given the complexity of the problems such a drastic decision entailed, in the end the two-year deadline was exceeded. The Catholic monarchs continued nonetheless to be strict in the confinement of the Jews. Their reason for creating such ghettos is easy to interpret. The monarchs saw this new requirement to completely separate Jews from the rest of the population as wholly consistent with their position with regard to the Jewish community. Through it, they were able to provide Jews with security and protection as subjects and vassals of the crown and confer them with a special status as an autonomous community within the kingdom.

If apartheid allowed for the enhanced protection of individuals and their property it also constituted a form of extreme discrimination and total segregation that ultimately shackled the development of normal, professional activities for Jews. In short, it made life impossible. It kept such pressure on Jews that the only way to return to a normal existence appeared to be to convert to Catholicism. Conversion was not specifically required—not yet—nor was their autonomous status affected, but the conditions were such that Jews were convinced that there was only one way out.

Authorities hoped to solve the problem of "judaicizing" new Christians by cutting off all relations between Jews and converts. They believed that as long as converts continued in contact with Jewish families and friends they would continue to observe Jewish custom and ritual and be vulnerable to outright Jewish proselytizing.[51] By completely separating Jews and Christians, Fernando and Isabel put an end to the enmity between new and old Christians that had contributed to political and social confrontations in the kingdom. Converts were to totally assimilate with, and solidly adhere to, Catholicism, and the constantly tense atmosphere was thus eliminated. All Christians were simply Christians; no other adjectives were required. In order to accomplish that, certain converts had to be persuaded to stop practicing any and all forms of Judaism.

The solution selected was to establish a regime of terror capable of intimidating the guilty and forewarning others. From the point of view of canon law, the "crypto-Jew" was a Christian heretic, that is, a member of the Church who disobeyed its dogma or rituals. The mentality at the time was that being a heretic was not only a personal sin but also constituted a danger for the rest of society whose cohesion would be threatened by such an infraction. A heretic thus deserved severe punishment.

In order to combat heresy in the twelfth century various European nations created special judges, called inquisitors, whose responsibility it was to inquire into—that is, to investigate—the truth of these acts, qualify them theologically, and pronounce the corresponding punishment if they indeed constituted a crime of heresy. These tribunals depended on ecclesiastical authority, in particular on the bishops' authority. In Castile there were no such tribunals. They were all located in the Kingdom of Aragon and not as inactive as has been purported. Between 1460 and 1467 at least fifteen trials were initiated against the crypto-Jews of Valencia.[52] It is not known whether these were effective means of stopping the practice. Almost all the treatises written on the subject in the previous reign had recommended very serious means of repressing false converts. For example, Brother de Espina wrote, "I believe that if in our time a veritable inquisition was made, there would be countless people to burn since so many [converts] are really practicing Judaism."[53] Alonso de Cartagena (*Defensorium unitatis christianae*) expressed a similar idea: "If some new Christian practices an evil custom. . . . may he be punished and reprimanded in a cruel manner and I will be the first to bring wood to burn him in the fire."

It is not surprising that many of these writers who wrote so critically of crypto-Jewish practices were themselves converts. In essence, what was at issue? The sincerity of some converts was placed in doubt, and they were accused of practicing Judaism—and indiscriminately referred to with the insulting term *Marranos*. From this point on, specific means were necessary to deal with the problem. The creation of a special jurisdiction was intended so a tribunal of justice could punish guilty crypto-Jews and save the honor of good Christians who were innocent of such crimes. Moreover, some converts hated Jews and false Christians to such an extent that they saw them as the main obstacle for their own complete assimilation into society.[54] Thus, Américo Castro's hypothesis (also expressed by Sánchez-Albornoz) on the origin of the Inquisition is not at all far-fetched.[55] It was an idea conceived of by converts.[56] Let us not forget the widespread custom in aljamas of excommunicating and punishing evil-doers for causing shame and damage to the community. The first general inquisitor, the famous Torquemada, was the nephew of a convert, Cardinal Juan de Torquemada.

During the reign of Enrique IV the Inquisition was at one point directed by Alonso de Espina and at another by the leader of the Dominicans, Brother Alonso de Oropesa, both probably converts. In 1461–62 Enrique IV requested the pope to authorize the designation of four inquisitors, two for Old Castile and two for New Castile and Andalusia, and asked that powers be delegated to the state to fight and repress heresy. The pope did not appear to understand fully what was being requested of him, or he acted as if that were the case. Instead, he designated a papal legate as inquisitor in Castile, who in turn was able to sub-delegate his powers to other ecclesiastical authorities, thereby introducing the equivalent of the so-called medieval Inquisition in Castile, albeit many years later.

It was not exactly what the king had asked in his petition, but Enrique IV did not insist. The noble faction opposing the king took the project on at its own behest. One of their demands presented in the Cigales [region] in the fall of 1464 was "that an inquisition of heretics and those suspected in matters of faith be made."[57] The same request was found in the sentence pronounced by arbitrators to reform the government of the kingdom in 1465, written in part by Brother de Oropesa. A doubt lingers, however, regarding the royal objective: Was it to create a new brand of tribunal named by the monarchy or to establish the episcopal inquisition as it was operating in other countries? In any event things did not proceed any further at the time. In this respect as in many others, it is interesting to note that Catholic monarchs made few if any innovations. They were content to appropriate an idea but with the firm aim of developing it and eliminating all obstacles to make it work.

No sooner was Isabel on the throne than she began to receive alarming information about the situation in Andalusia from Brother Alonso de Ojeda, the Dominican prior of the Convent of San Pablo of Seville. In Seville, many converts who held public office or positions within the Church were practicing Judaism almost openly. They were respecting the Sabbath, circumcising their children, eating meat on days prohibited by the Church, reciting Jewish prayers, celebrating Passover and other Jewish holidays, and burying their dead in the Jewish way. During their visit to Andalusia in 1477–78 Isabel and Fernando collected additional testimony and personally observed the situation regarding religious practices in that area.[58]

Returning to Seville, the monarchs initiated their negotiations with Rome in order to obtain papal authorization to name inquisitors in their kingdom. Unlike previous inquisitions delegated to officials of the Church, the monarchs requested that the pope delegate the power to run judicial procedures against heretics to the crown. Times had changed since Enrique IV. The new sovereigns tenaciously procured prerogatives for the monarchy and expanded upon them. They did not allow Rome's direct interference in matters of internal government. Each nomination of a bishop was cause for diplomatic confrontations until the monarchs could personally designate clergy of their choice. Sixtus IV wanted to avoid additional conflicts with the Catholic monarchs and acceded to their demand in the bull he signed on November 1, 1478, *Exigit sincerae devotionis,* which authorized Isabel and Fernando to name inquisitors.

The Catholic monarchs did not immediately use that right. For almost two years they were under strong pressure from members of the clergy who were among their most respected advisors, in particular Brother Hernando de Talavera, the queen's confessor, and Cardinal Mendoza, who held great influence in court and was directly concerned because he was archbishop of Seville, an area highly implicated in conversion scandals. From the beginning, Talavera and Mendoza were aware of and appalled by the cruelty of religious repression. They obtained from the monarchs the role of developing an intensive campaign of catechism aimed at instructing converts in their obligations. They attempted to convince converts of the necessity of definitively breaking all ties with Judaism and with all beliefs, rites, and customs that were not in conformity with the teachings and dogma of the Church.

Cardinal Mendoza wrote a catechism that was distributed in all the archbishopric's churches. A pastoral sermon, it ordered the clergy to dedicate their efforts to the religious instruction of the faithful and pay special attention to new Christians. As for Talavera, he gave sermons in Seville in 1478 to demonstrate the "very higher excellence of the Holy Gospel. . . . in relation to the Old Testament, law of the letter, of shadow and figure. . . . and how the orders, ceremonies, observations, and judgments of the former ended with the coming of our Lord Jesus Christ and by the spreading of his Holy Gospel." Thus Talavera suggested a few ordinances to Cardinal Mendoza "so that Christian religion and life may flourish. . . . in that very noble city and in its territories that were defiled by the newly converted, those of waning Catholic faith who [continued to] observe Jewish rites and ceremonies.[59]

Talavera and Mendoza were very conscious of the gravity of the task at hand. The reality of many Andalusian converts' crypto-Judaism did not escape them, but they considered that repression was not the appropriate solution. Their view was that converts had received insufficient religious education—in fact, sometimes none at all. If new converts' errors could be attributed more to ignorance than to maliciousness then it would be unjust to take harsh measures against them without an attempt to instruct them and convince them to abandon their Jewish practices.

That campaign came late. "It achieved little" as the journalist Pulgar stated, himself a convert hostile to the planned Inquisition. Diego de Merlo, assistant bishop in Seville, realized that the catechism and sermons had gained no tangible results at all. The false converts practicing Judaism did not believe that they would be struck down from above. Not only did they ignore the sermons, catechisms, and other means of evangelization, but also some of them got together to write a tract to justify their position. They affirmed that nothing was contradictory in the simultaneous practice of the law of Moses and Christianity. Because the latter perfected the former, they reasoned that they therefore had to, or at least if they could, should maintain some practices from Mosaic law along with the precepts of the Holy Gospel. The tract's authors went even further in ridiculing old Christians and affirming the intellectual superiority of converts who also practiced Judaism. They wrote, "Because Jewish converts are knowledgeable and highly ingenious people, they cannot, and do not want to implicate themselves in the mockery believed in and created by the Gentile (pagan) converts to Catholicism."[60]

In other words, the rites of traditional Catholicism were fine for the simple-minded, but Jewish converts, who were more intelligent, could not swallow such nonsense. The time could not have been less opportune for such imprudent and insulting declarations. Such unawareness of possible repercussions can only be explained by the zeal with which some manifested their materialist beliefs and lack of faith in religious dogma. To make matters worse, the tract ended with personal attacks against Talavera, adding nothing to the core of the debate but hurting and destabilizing one of the most tolerant evangelists of the period. This all became more than clear a few years later when, as archbishop of the new dioceses of conquered Granada, Talavera's apostolate used gentle persuasion to convince the Moorish population. Talavera's conclusion in *Católica impugnación* was a defense of the Inquisition: "It is true that those who secretly practice Judaism [*judaizantes*] should in some cases be put to death, as prescribed by canon law and civil law."

The die was cast. The Catholic monarchs, who until then had wavered, decided to use the powers they had received through the papal bull of 1478. On

September 27, 1480, they named the first inquisitors, who began their work in Seville two months later, spreading terror in their paths. Hundreds of converts—Bernáldez speaks of some eight thousand—escaped the city to seek refuge on nobles' lands. This was of no use to them in the end. A royal order dated January 1, 1481, warned the Andalusian magnates not to circumvent inquisitorial justice. Such an infringement would be equated with disobeying the monarchy, and such obvious contempt would lead to severe punishments. Those who tried to resist inquisitors by force or conspired to prevent their actions would be arrested, condemned to death, and executed.

Detentions and trials began. Sanctions rained upon the population. Seven hundred death sentences and more than five thousand "reconciliations" (that is, prison sentences, orders for exile, or simple penances) were pronounced between 1481 and 1488 in the city of Seville alone. In Guadalupe in seven trials in 1485, fifty-two death sentences were pronounced, of which more than forty-six were posthumous and twenty-five were in effigy. In addition, seventeen life-term prison sentences were decreed. All the condemnations were accompanied by a confiscation of all property and stripping away any public office or ecclesiastical benefit the false convert may have enjoyed. The inquisitors were not content to detain and condemn those who practiced Judaism. They did not forget that their objective was to assimilate the converts. Yet they believed that such assimilation would remain difficult as long as the example of practicing Jews existed. They therefore requested and obtained in 1483 the expulsion of Andalusian Jews from the dioceses of Seville, Cádiz, and Córdoba over a period of six months.[61] An attempt was made to prevent all communication and any contact between converts and Jews.

The 1483 expulsion measure was thus the immediate precedent to the expulsion of 1492. It showed that the Inquisition and the expulsion were two sides of the same coherent political coin—putting an end to peninsular Judaism. The harshness of Seville's inquisitors upset many people, both converts and others. Although some agreed with the principle of sanctioning heretics, most were afraid of what was happening in the process. They attempted to convince the monarchs to use less violent means:

> They said the same thing [some of the relatives of the arrested and condemned] that in the manner of having the trials and obtaining testimony and information and the tortures they used and in the execution of sentences and other circumstances, the ecclesiastical inquisitors and secular executors acted with cruelty. They acted with great malice, not only against those they sentenced and tortured, but against everyone, since they were imbued with mission of marking with infamy any who would be guilty of that horrible crime. And [especially] considering the piety of God and how the Holy Mother Church recommends

responding in such cases, [that is] with gentle reasoning, temperate warnings, good doctrines and examples to bring the errant into the faith. To follow the precepts and rules of the holy canons, they should reduce the punishments the laws prescribe and disallow that cruel punishment by burning. Especially [no such punishment should be used], if they confess their error and convert to the faith of Christ, Our Redeemer, because they say that it was an inhuman and cruel thing to burn someone who calls out in the name of Christ and confesses the Christian faith and wants to live like a Christian.[62]

The Inquisition's adversaries also protested against a fundamental problem, the discrimination that converts suffered. In short, "They said that the papal bull concerning this matter included only converted Christians of Jewish descent and not any others, whence it was clear that the prosecutor who enacted it wanted to tarnish all those of that lineage, making that bull their specialty and no one else's."[63]

In fact, the bull creating the Inquisition established an inadmissible discrimination between heretics. The Holy Office, by attacking one category of heresy—that of Jewish practitioners and heresies based on those of Jewish ascendancy—went against the basic principles of the universality of Catholicism: the Church is a single flock of sheep with one pastor in Jesus Christ.

Such blatant discrimination leaves the true intentions of the inquisitors in doubt. Under the pretext of punishing those Christian converts who practiced Judaism, were they not trying to defame and destroy all converts, Jewish practitioners or not? As soon as one opts to persecute this single category of heretics, all converts, by virtue of being converts, become virtual criminals, suspects, and pariahs. History later confirmed that prediction. Spaniards of Jewish origin would continue to feel that their lives, possessions, and honor were threatened. Soon, rules were established to require everyone who applied for certain honors, prebends, or benefits (for example, habits of the military orders, cathedral chapters, religious orders, brotherhoods, and positions in major colleges) to prove that neither they nor their fathers or grandfathers or great-grandfathers had been persecuted or punished by the Holy Office. In a systematic manner, all those with a Jewish past were distrusted. On the fringes of the Spanish Inquisition something akin to what Pero Sarmiento had proposed back in 1449 began to be enacted throughout the country—cleansing of blood.

The Catholic monarchs did not cede to the scruples or warnings of Sixtus IV, who, alerted by informants of what was happening in Spain, attempted to hide behind the fact that the new inquisitorial tribunal escaped Church control. It was true that the royal powers named the inquisitors, that they depended exclusively on the monarchy, and that their only responsibility was to give accounts to the bishops. The pope therefore decided to annul his bull of 1478 and attempted to entrust the Inquisition to the bishops, whose prerogatives were disregarded by the inquisitors. Usually, when a priest gave absolution the accused could not be judged. The monarchs, however, resolutely opposed this practice, and Sixtus IV provided a temporary solution. Inquisitors would continue their work and keep giving detailed accounts to the bishops, but the condemned could make an appeal of their sentences before Rome. This was not a success, either. King Fernando demanded that things continue as they had been, and Sixtus IV abandoned his opposition to the monarch. On February 25, 1483, he confirmed the 1478 bull with a single added restriction: The Archbishop of Seville would be able to learn of the sentences as they were decided.

At the end of 1488 a group of converts made a new attempt with Sixtus IV's successor, Innocent VIII. Once again they failed. The crown continued to name inquisitors, and all trials took place and were judged in Spain with no possibility of appealing to Rome. Even more flagrant, the Catholic monarchs threatened with death anyone who would use papal dispensations or absolutions to circumvent the Inquisition. The monarchy maintained total control in repressing heresy. The only concession made by the Catholic monarchs was to allow an appeal to Rome when bishops were implicated in a trial. While these discussions were developing with Rome, King Ferdinand had inherited the Crown of Aragon in 1479. Because the papal bull of 1478 was only valid in Castile, Ferdinand made a formal request to the Holy Office to allow him to establish the Inquisition in Aragon. He came out on top, personally pushing the Inquisition into the Kingdom of Aragon against all possible resistance.

The Expulsion

On November 16, 1491, during an auto-da-fé in Avila, the Inquisition sentenced five people to death, and two Jews and three converts were burned alive on the spot. This was the tragic end to a mysterious case that had begun in June of the previous year with the fortuitous detention in Astorga of one Benito García, a convert suspected of stealing sacred hosts. García confessed that since 1485 he had been practicing Judaism under the influence of other converts, namely the families of Juan de Ocaña and Franco de Tembleque. García was then incarcerated in the Inquisition's prison in Segovia, where Yucé Franco, a Jewish shoemaker, was also being held.

In principle, the Inquisition had no authority over Jews because its jurisdiction only extended to the baptized. What then was a Jew doing in the inquisitorial prison in Segovia? This is only one of the many enigmas pertaining to the case of the Holy Child of La Guardia. The complicated story also involved another Jew, Dr. Antonio de Avila, who, posing as a rabbi, came to visit Yucé Franco, who then confessed to having committed a heinous crime some fifteen years earlier. Franco first stated that on Good Friday in the town of La Guardia in the province of Toledo, he had participated in a ritual crime. He murdered a child by crucifixion and then mixed the victim's blood and heart with a holy host in an act of witchcraft aimed at provoking an epidemic of rabies throughout the land. Denounced by the pseudo-rabbi (perhaps an infiltrator paid by the Inquisition), Franco later recanted, claiming never to have participated in any crime himself. Instead, he changed his statement, saying that he had merely heard of this crime from a convert in La Guardia named Alonso Franco. Under torture, however, Yucé Franco returned to his original confession and again admitted his participation in the crime.

After these revelations the Inquisition detained several converts and im-

prisoned them in Avila. We also might wonder, why Avila? Why were they
not taken to Toledo, the closest main city to La Guardia? This, too, remains
an enigma. The formal trial began on December 17, 1490, and ended a year
later, resulting in the guilty verdict and death sentence for five of the accused.
Everything in the trial proceedings rings false. No one knew who the child was
or who his parents were, and, apparently, no one presented any formal accusation. The declarations and confessions were incoherent and contradictory.
Recent investigations of the case have not cleared up the mystery. It appears
obvious that the Inquisition concocted the matter as a provocation, but for
what purpose? Probably, it was intended to heat up public opinion against Jews
and converts, perhaps to justify increasing repressive measures. If that were so,
those responsible actually failed at the task. In contemporary literature there is
no mention of the event, nor is it referred to in the edict expelling the Jews.

There were three different versions of the expulsion edict that was presented in legal terms as a royal decree:

—One by the inquisitor general, Torquemada, dated March 20 in Santa Fe, that
is, ten days before the monarchs' official decree by the Bishop of Gerona;[1]
—a second decree, signed on March 31 in Granada by Don Fernando and Doña
Isabel for the Kingdom of Castile;[2]
—and a third decree, a much lesser-known text, also dated March 31 in Granada
but with Don Fernando's signature alone and valid for the Kingdom of Aragon.[3]

It is clear that Torquemada's text was used as the basic document for the
other two. This demonstrates the Inquisition's lead role in the expulsion, a fact
openly declared in the Aragonese version of the edict.[4] The monarchs, however, must have judged his edict excessive because the Inquisition's jurisdiction
concerned Christians, more specifically converts, but not Jews. The Aragonese
decree reaffirmed the official position: Jews "are ours." In other words, only
the crown could decide their fate.

Significant differences can be noted in comparing the three versions. Torquemada's and the Castilian version are strictly limited to the religious issues and
contain no references to usury. Torquemada's version is the most injurious of
the three; it accuses Jews of mocking Christian laws and treats them as idolaters. Such language is absent from the Castilian version. Torquemada's decree
adds nine more days to the deadline set for the expulsion (end of July). As it
turned out, nine days were added to the deadline, but the extension was never
mentioned in the other two later documents. Once again, this demonstrates
that Torquemada's Inquisition was the protagonist in the implementation of
the expulsion. The Aragonese version is the harshest of the three, especially in

terms of style.[5] This text cites that Jews "for their own fault" are "to submit to perpetual subjugation" as "servants and captives." Most notably, the Aragonese version referred to religious motives and the theme of usury.[6]

The Castilian version is the most austere. The first half of the text exposes the problem that the presence of Jews created among Christians on Spanish soil. Communication between converts and Jews is noted as the main cause of the problem. The document then reviews the measures enacted by the monarchs since coming to the throne: (a) requiring Jews to live in separate neighborhoods (Cortes de Toledo, 1480); (b) creating, also in 1480, the Inquisition tribunal whose original mission it was to curtail various forms of Jewish apostasy; and, finally, (c) expelling the Jews from Andalusia in 1483. Deeming these previously attempted measures as insufficient, the monarchs then decided to eliminate the main causal agent by expelling all Jews. Although it was admitted that by acting in this manner innocent Jews would suffer severe prejudice, the edict underscored the collective responsibility of the entire Hebrew community: "When a serious and heinous crime is committed by some members of a given college and university [this should be understood as meaning of any corporation or collective body], it is reasonable that that college or university be dissolved and disbanded, and the minors along with the majors, and each and every one be punished."

The second half of the edict specifies how the expulsion was to be implemented:

1. The expulsion was definitive: "we agree to send out all Jewish men and women from our kingdoms and that they should never return to any one of them."
2. No exceptions were to be made; the law was to apply to all Jews, regardless of age, including all naturalized individuals, those born in Spain, and all foreign Jews who, for whatever reason, were residing in Spain, that is, living in the Catholic monarchs' kingdoms and dominions, that is, in all parts of Castile, the Kingdom of Aragon, and annexed territories.
3. The expulsion was to take effect at the end of July. A period of four months was set aside, after which it became irreversible. Those who did not leave by the end of the four-month period would incur the death penalty and be liable to the confiscation of all their possessions. Any non-Jews who would offer asylum to Jews, hide them, or abet them in avoiding compliance with the expulsion edict would also be liable to the loss of "all their possessions, vassals, strongholds and other inheritance." As mentioned, Torquemada's earlier version of the decree had also added ten more days to the deadline for expulsion, effectively extending it to August 10.
4. During the period set aside for the expulsion, Jews were allowed to sell their belongings and properties but with certain restrictions.
5. The previously legislated bans against the export of gold, silver, and minted

money were maintained. Jews, however, were able to obtain letters of credit or merchandise except for regularly prohibited items such as arms and horses.

The edict was not made public until the end of April. Possibly, the delay was due to several attempts made to revoke or attenuate the expulsion of the Jews. We know that Isaac ben Yedudá Abravanel made such an attempt without success.[7]

The deadline for the departure was strictly maintained. Nothing in the edict specifically mentioned any possibility of converting before the expulsion date, so, formally speaking, authors who present the decision of 1492 as a choice between exile or conversion err. In reality, however, conversion was understood as the alternative because only Jews were forced into exile. Those concerned clearly understood that if they decided to convert to Christianity at the last minute they would not be affected by the edict. The most famous case is that of Abraham Seneor, rab mayor of Castile, the prominent leader of the Jewish community and close and faithful collaborator of the crown. He, his son-in-law Mayr Melamed, and all their relatives received baptism on June 15, 1492, in the monastery of Guadalupe in a ceremony in which the sovereign rulers, King Fernando and Queen Isabel, acted as godparents. Abraham Seneor consequently changed his name to Fernán Núñez Coronel. Some days later he was named as the *regidor* (governor) of Segovia, a member of the Royal Council, and major accountant for Prince Don Juan. His son-in-law was given the name Fernán Pérez Coronel. Note that both of their baptismal names were taken from that of their godfather, the king.[8] Fifteen days earlier, on May 31, another prominent Jew, Abraham de Córdoba, was baptized, with Cardinal Mendoza and the papal nuncio acting as godfathers.

It is clear that a few spectacular conversions, and the publicity surrounding them, did much to convince the majority of Jews to follow suit. Indeed, there were many conversions in those months. Baer states that conversions were especially numerous among the wealthy and intellectuals, those "corrupted by secular culture," or rather among those belonging to the Jewish social elite.[9] Isaac Abravanel was the only financier of importance who decided to follow fellow Jews into exile.[10] The vast majority of rabbis converted to Christianity according to a contemporary Jewish source. "Those who had little departed and the others stayed" wrote a chronicler from Jerez.[11] Andrés Bernáldez gives testimony to the intense propaganda campaign that followed:

In all the aljamas and [Jewish] communities, the wise men of Spain gave many sermons in all the synagogues and in all the squares, churches and [throughout] the country; they preached the Holy Gospel and the doctrine of the Holy Mother Church [which was] made evident by the very same Scriptures; the Messiah whom they awaited was our Redeemer and Our Savior Jesus Christ, who came at the appointed time, who ignored their former sin, and [yet] all the others who came afterwards never wanted to listen to the truth; before they were tricked by the false book of the Talmud, [although they had] the truth before their eyes and read it in their law every day, they used to ignore it and did ignore it.[12]

In a single morning a hundred men, women, and children were baptized in Teruel. Governors even went from house to house to convince the Jews to convert to Christianity to be able to remain in Spain because their departure was feared tantamount to the city's ruination.[13] They did not always get the results for which they hoped. The Duke del Infantado, a Mendoza, attempted in various ways to encourage the conversion of his Jewish subjects from Maqueda and Torrijos, one of the most important aljamas in his territories and in the entire kingdom. His efforts were in vain. Nonetheless, there were indeed last-minute conversions: "Some Jews, when the time limit was up, went around day and night in desperation. Many returned from the road. . . . and received the faith of Christ. Many others were baptized to avoid being bereft of the land in which they were born and in order to avoid liquidating their possessions."[14]

With their hopes dashed that the monarchs would change their mind, Jews had to prepare for the long road ahead in terrible conditions. "They sold and undersold," wrote Bernáldez, "as much as they could of their houses and properties. . . . and had no luck with any of it; Christians procured their properties, very many very rich houses and inherited possessions, for very little money. Jews went around begging Christians, and when they could find no buyers, they gave a house away for a donkey, or a vineyard for a little cloth or linen, because they were not allowed to carry gold or silver with them." The monarchs named commissioners to check the economic effects of the expulsion with an inventory of property, goods, annuities, pensions, and debts. Notwithstanding, everything took place with a great deal of improvisation due to the mad rush. Given the approaching deadline, Jews were not able to sell their houses and land for a fair price and had to content themselves with ridiculously low sums offered in exchange for much more valuable goods. Jews could then buy goods to take with them whose export was authorized. They could also carry letters of credit to foreign places, but these were ultimately of little help because bankers, especially Italian bankers, took advantage of the situation by charging them increased interest rates. There were Jews who mocked the prohibition against taking gold abroad and were able to take money with the complicity of royal officials and nobles. Others did the same with contraband. Bernáldez recounts that some people, especially women, swallowed coins before arriving at the border: "It happened that some people would swallow up to thirty coins at a time."

The aljamas were supposed to sell community goods—synagogues and land—in order to cover the expenses of the poorest en route to exile. In places such as Palencia, however, the council prohibited the purchase of such community goods. Judizmendi's lands in Vitoria led to an emotional transaction. The aljama ceded the property to the council on the condition that it would forever after serve only as a pasture. That was because the Jewish cemetery was situated on this piece of land, and the aljama wanted to prevent the property from being profaned.[15]

It was exceedingly difficult for Jews to recover debts from Christians. Christians had fifteen days to prove the rightfulness of their claims to any holdings left by expelled Jews. Many complaints and lawsuits were not settled in a satisfactory manner or left unresolved. There were, for example, sometimes loans or credits that did not come due until after the August 10 deadline for the expulsion, and they were turned over to Christian creditors who promised to cover the debts. Yet many debtors refused to pay on the pretext that the debts were "frauds of usury." The Royal Council had to intervene in order to resolve matters rapidly although that was not always possible. In certain cases the monarchs were magnanimous and showed clemency. As a tax collector, Isaac Abravanel owed the Royal Treasury more than a million maravedís and handed over receipts to the crown, to be used later. In gratitude for his service to the monarchy he was given special permission to take gold, money, and jewelry in the amount of some one thousand ducats.

The cruel moment finally arrived when Jews had to leave the country they had lived in for centuries. Bernáldez relates that

> all the young men and young women over twelve years of age were married to each other, because at the time wives were protected and accompanied by their husbands [when they traveled]. . . . Young and old, children and adults, by foot and on donkeys and other beasts, and in carriage carts, they left the land of their birth. Each of them was headed for the ports from which they were to depart. They went by way of roads and fields where they used to go to work and earn their living. Some of them were falling down, others getting up, some dying and others being born and some were very sick; there was no Christian who did not feel pain for them. Wherever they went, they were invited to be baptized and some, in misery, converted and remained, but very few, and the rabbis encouraged them and had the women and young people sing and play tambourines.

Isaac Abravanel spent practically the entire time allotted organizing the departure. With the help of a royal official, Luis de Santángel, and the Genovese banker Francisco Pinelo, Abravanel contracted boats. In some cases the monarchs issued orders to protect Jews up to the border or the port of embarkation.[16] In that painfully critical moment Jews were also vulnerable to all kinds of extortion and abuse. All expenses of the expulsion were being born by the departing Jews, including travel costs, provisions, freight for the boats, and rights of passage. They contracted for, at inflated rates, ships whose owners on more than one occasion neglected to fulfill their commitments. Other departing Jews were murdered and robbed of their possessions.

How many left Spain at the time of the expulsion? The estimates range between 40,000 and 350,000. Bernáldez speaks of some 170,000 fleeing Jews. Recent research based on reliable sources approximates a total of fewer than fifty thousand, taking into account those who returned. It is difficult to specify exactly how many there were who did so. Luis Suárez Fernández managed to list 177 names, for the most part heads of household, which implies that the actual numbers were much greater.[17] Many who left for Fez preferred to return to Spain due to the poor treatment they received there, and they asked the governor of Arcila to baptize them. On November 10, 1492, those cases had to be addressed, and church and civil authorities had to attest to the baptism of those who had converted in Spain. Had a conversion taken place abroad, proof and witnesses were required to confirm it. In such cases Jews were to be able to retrieve possessions for the same price at which they sold them. Documentation regarding such returns exists from at least 1499. Those who returned were encouraged to assimilate with Christians and receive adequate religious instruction.[18] Moreover, the Royal Council's decree of October 24, 1493, threatened serious sanctions against any who insulted the new Christians, for example, by calling them "turncoats."[19]

In general, the expelled Jews left for Mediterranean areas or nearby countries where their living conditions were not that different from those in Spain. It seems that very few left for Northern Europe (England or Flanders). The Álava Jews went to Navarre but were expelled from there in 1498. They then moved to France, where they founded the neighborhood of the Holy Spirit in Bayonne. Jews from the Kingdom of Aragon went to Navarre or Tortosa to embark. Most Castilian Jews went to Portugal, where King Juan II authorized a six-month stay in exchange for a ducat coin. Many stayed much longer, until such time as they were expelled from there as well. From there they left for North Africa, where other Jews had already arrived directly from Cádiz.[20] In the Kingdom of Fez they were poorly received and mercilessly plundered not only by Muslims but also by Arabic-speaking Jews who had long lived in that country. It is understandable that many would have preferred to return to Spain.

Those who went to Italy (Rome, Ferrara, and Venice) had better luck where, paradoxically, they made the most of being Spanish. They sought out the company of Spanish nobles and gentlemen, thereby contributing to the idea current in sixteenth-century Italy that Spaniards were Jews. For others, Italy was a mere stopover on the road leading to the East toward Salonika, Constantinople, Smyrna, Rhodes, Monastir, Sarajevo, and Sofia.

Turkey was the only great power that welcomed Jews with open arms. Sultan Bayazet II wrote to all his representatives, instructing that Jews be well received and helped to settle on Turkish land. It is said that his successor, Suleiman, exclaimed on one occasion, referring to Don Fernando, "Is this the king you call such a good politician who impoverishes his states to enrich mine?" Brother Diego de Mérida, a priest from the Monastery of Guadalupe, visited the region some twenty years later and published his *Voyage to the Orient* in 1512. In it he recounts how he met some Jews from Seville in Bethlehem: "As soon as they saw us priests, they longed for Seville and for the mincemeat balls and [traditional Jewish] stew they used to make in Seville." He also relates that at the Saint Mark's luncheon in Egypt, he bumped into a Mameluke, originally from Seville, who explained to him that: "Of the twenty thousand existing Mamelukes, if the king of Spain or France came to the area, half would turn back, for they desire nothing else."[21] In 1518 Brother García Jofre de Loaisa, knight of the Order of San Juan, was sent by Carlos I to petition Suleiman not to mistreat pilgrims coming to Jerusalem. The sultan answered that he would be happy to comply, adding "that he was surprised that they had expelled the Jews from Castile, since it [amounted to] throwing away wealth."[22]

The Ottoman Empire was a second homeland for Spanish Jews. Although subjected to oppression and significant fiscal pressure, they could nevertheless continue practicing their religion, given the Turks' relative tolerance in matters of religion. Jews [in Turkey] have thus maintained many ancestral customs up through the modern age, in particular they have continued to speak Spanish. The Spanish they use is not exactly that of fifteenth-century Spain, but as with all living languages it has evolved and significantly changed over the years although the structures and essential characteristics are those of early medieval Spanish.

Thus the Sephardic communities of Europe were born in the Mediterranean area, in Flanders, in southeastern France, in North Africa, and in the Middle East. As of the sixteenth century the population of these communities grew with the emigration of crypto-Jews fleeing the Inquisition. In the twentieth century, Jewish folklorists and scholars have written stories and sung ballads of ancient Spain, thus preserving history through the oral tradition. Although the Sephardim have never forgotten the land of their forebears they have continued to have mixed feelings about it. On one hand there has been resentment for the tragic events of 1492, and on the other a persistent longing and homesickness. That nostalgia, documented for the first years of the sixteenth century, continued to grow.

Hence the year 1492 signals the end of Spanish Judaism, for its ensuing existence was to be relegated to an underground phenomenon. Judaism remained threatened by the inquisitorial apparatus and public mistrust. Jews, false converts, and even sincere converts continued to be viewed as the natural enemies of Catholicism and the Spanish "identity" as church leaders and intellectuals understood and imposed it. There is little doubt that this attitude bordered on racism, but it still remains to be seen what motivated the Catholic monarchs to employ such drastic means. Much ink has been wasted in such an attempt, and all kinds of interpretations have been proposed, some of which are frankly unfounded. We can categorize all these interpretations and group them according to a few main themes in answer to the question, Why did Fernando and Isabel finally resort to expelling the Jews?

In the first place, we must eliminate the most simplistic response. It was not the sovereigns' greed compelled by financial necessities to usurp Jewish wealth. That hypothesis does not hold up under examination. As subjects and vassals of the crown, Jews depended on it completely. They had no institutions like the Christians' parliament to establish certain limits on royal power, albeit theoretical and very relative but effective. Jews had no guarantees. Sovereign leaders could demand of them whatever their whims dictated, and they did so in various circumstances throughout the Middle Ages and during the era of the Catholic monarchs, with the War of Granada, for example, as a pretext. It is not clear what the monarchs might have gained by dispossessing Jews at the time of the expulsion. Although the edict profited unscrupulous individuals who bought up valuable Jewish possessions for little money and committed many other abuses, the crown did not appear to have profited much from the operation. Jews were of interest more as taxpayers, but taxes disappeared with the expulsion of taxpayers. As Antonio Domínguez Ortíz said on one occasion, the best way to establish a tax on capital is not to eliminate capitalism and capitalists. That would be akin to killing the golden goose. The expulsion obliged Jews to undersell their possessions in a few weeks and under very risky conditions, but it in no way signified a confiscation benefiting the crown. Of course, the crown required Jews to pay any outstanding debts but did not take advantage of the occasion to dispossess them.[23]

Moreover, the Jews' importance in economic life and their role as the driving force of budding capitalism have been much exaggerated. At the time of the expulsion this importance and role were no longer what they had once been, if indeed the same was not true in previous eras. Given the published documentation concerning fiscal matters and economic activities there is not the slightest doubt that Jews no longer constituted a source of relevant wealth; few were still bankers, tax collectors, or merchants developing business at an international level. That is what the situation of 1492 confirmed in years that followed.

The expulsion led to various upheavals in economic life in many areas. Over night, people had to do without specific artisans or merchants. Taxes and rents were significantly lowered, as documented by Juan de Mata Carriazo in the case of Seville and as can be ascertained for many other places. It is true that economic difficulties had already begun a decade earlier with the establishment of the Inquisition.[24] The effect of an eroded tax base was already felt in Zamora, Barcelona, and many other cities.

King Fernando and Queen Isabel were aware that their politics concerning the Jews and converts might lead to negative consequences of this kind, but they subordinated everything to the mission they had set out to accomplish.[25] This demonstrates that nations do not always determine their conduct according to mere economics. Under certain conditions they deliberately sacrifice these interests to concentrate on other objectives, including ideological ones, that seem to merit all their attention, whatever the cost.[26]

In many ways expulsion of the Jews gave rise to problems on a local level but did not produce a national catastrophe. It is, in every respect, groundless to attribute the expulsion to the decadence of Spain and its supposed incapacity to adapt to the transformations of the modern world. All information presently available demonstrates that sixteenth-century Spain was not an economically backward nation. Its demographic and commercial might was forged in previous years, and expansion continued at least until the end of the century. The expulsion of Jews—unlike that of Moors at the beginning of the seventeenth century—occurred at the height of prosperity. In strictly demographic and economic terms, and excluding the human dimension, the expulsion did not substantially harm Spain but rather constituted a passing crisis that was rapidly overcome.[27]

Another interpretation holds that in many instances Jews had been driven out by converts not implicated by the edict of 1492. Partisans of that thesis emphasize that Jews could not be clearly separated from converts because both groups were united in the face of a common persecution. The former were exiled, and the latter were subject to the Inquisition. This valid argument leads to a broader, more materialist, and now familiar interpretation of events. The expulsion can thus be viewed as another episode of class struggle between two groups, the traditionally privileged class and the emerging middle class. Henry

Kamen developed this fundamentally Marxist thesis some years ago in connection with the events of 1492.[28] This broad interpretation holds that the expulsion was inspired by the feudal nobility, who wanted to eliminate a sector of the growing middle class—Jews—who threatened its ambition to dominate and control the state. The nobility, by definition, a privileged, land-owning class of society with power based on inherited wealth, reacted against the growing influence of the social class that relied on capital and economic activities. From that perspective the defense of the faith and orthodoxy was nothing more than an ideological mask that concealed more concrete objectives. The punishments pronounced by the Inquisition against those practicing Judaism included death sentences, the confiscation of goods, and a ban on holding public offices, but in reality the Inquisition had acted to threaten all converts and eliminate a rival class, the growing bourgeoisie (townspeople, that is, the people of Burgos). Expulsion of the Jews would then be the logical and chronological extension of the creation of the Holy Office because both measures pursued the same ends.[29]

Matters, however, are not that unambiguous. It would be absurd to contend that the Catholic monarchs' religious politics were motivated solely by the realm of pure ideas with no admixture of material considerations. Many issues were at play in addition to concrete interests, particularly the emerging concept of what the modern state was meant to be. In and of itself the interpretation of specific events in terms of class struggle is generally acceptable, but everything depends on situations that class struggle is supposed to explain. Can the Inquisition and the expulsion of the Jews be explained as episodes of class struggle? An affirmative response implies two prior conditions:

1. that classes exist; and
2. that these classes were in opposition.

We consider it a given that the nobility constituted a social class in spite of the different levels that may have existed within it: very wealthy men known in the sixteenth century as the great ones (*los grandes*), lords (*hidalgos*), and gentlemen (*caballeros*). It certainly constituted a social class even though ambition for power and wealth occasioned internal oppositions pitting its members against one another. During the fifteenth century Castilian nobility continued to be a fundamentally land-owning class, possessing extensive feudal domains and receiving substantial rents. The Catholic monarchs' reorganization of the Courts of Toledo in 1480 curtailed many abuses but left the nobility with economic importance and social prestige.

In Spanish society of the period there was also a middle class, a bourgeoisie whose fortunes had been made in peninsular and especially international commerce and who had begun to be involved in manufacturing enterprises.

Were all those people Jews or converts? No. At the time of the expulsion Jews did not constitute a powerful middle class because the great majority of them were modest artisans, shopkeepers, and small-time moneylenders. Equating Jews with the bourgeoisie is unfounded. Historical social research has rejected that theory of the Jewish origins of capitalism and the monetary economy. In the case of Spain, much was based on the idea of the supposed incapacity of the Spanish for economic activities. The fact is that not all Jews and converts were part of a growing middle class. More to the point, although some belonged to the bourgeoisie they were by no means the only ones who did.

Did middle-class Jews constitute a threat to the Spanish nobility? The documentation available tends to indicate much the opposite. It signals the presence of Jews in feudal courts, where they occupied such financial positions as tax collector and treasurer. In other words they worked in the service of, and collaboration with, the grandees who needed them. These noble lords were the first to be directly disadvantaged by the expulsion because many aljamas were located on their land and contributed to their prosperity.[30] Moreover, it is a proven fact that many magnates protected converts and Jews who felt more secure living in their domains. As soon as the Inquisition was established in Seville many converts fled to take refuge in territories belonging to the Duke of Medina Sidonia, the Count of Niebla, and other powerful lords.

The edict of 1492 accurately foresaw that some Jews would try to escape the expulsion order by placing themselves under the protection of landed nobility. It therefore placed anyone who tried to help Jews under penalty of confiscation of their goods, including their subjects, castles, inheritance, and belongings. If only for this mention we realize that the Catholic monarchs suspected a possible intervention of the nobility in favor of the Jews.

A later episode also helps elucidate the problem. The *comunera* (popular) revolution was, in my view, born of a clearly modern spirit. It attempted to change profoundly the political order of the kingdom, introducing a form of control over royal power. It was, if one prefers, a bourgeois movement or at least a middle-class phenomenon. The comunera revolution failed because it clashed with the nobility's opposition and with that of the authentic bourgeoisie. Their defection from Burgos and adhesion to the governors was a severe blow to the Tordesillas Junta, one from which it was never able to recover. On this occasion the bourgeois patrons of great international commerce were aligned with the magnates of noble extraction. Their interests were complementary. For the nobility, owners of fields and pastures, it was of interest to maintain the production of merino wool, which salesmen from Burgos traded abroad. There is no more evident case of political solidarity based on complementary economic interests. It would therefore be erroneous to see Castilian nobility and the middle class at the end of the fifteenth and beginning of the sixteenth centuries as antagonistic. Everything points to the contrary.

S. H. Haliczer proposes a variant of the class war thesis.[31] The nobility was not the class to have attempted to eliminate Jews, but rather it was the traditional bourgeoisie—in other words and more precisely, the urban oligarchy. These people had supported the Catholic monarchs during the War of Succession, thereby acceding to positions of power. In exchange, Halcizer holds that they required and obtained the expulsion of Jews. It is true that various councils and the parliament, basically urban, popular assemblies, were consistently hostile to Jews and often requested reinstatement of previous discriminatory measures against them, in particular the application of the laws against usury. It so happens that within the urban oligarchy, well-represented in parliament, there were many who owed money to Jewish lenders on both individual and collective levels, the latter, for example, as members of the councils (*regimientos*). That is why some urban oligarchs expended such energy in attempting to ban or regulate against what they called usury.[32]

From 1480 onward the crown satisfied those demands for debt recovery and put strict measures into practice. Haliczer's thesis does not, however, take into account two aspects of the problem. First, the expulsion came to complete the measure initiated with the creation of the Inquisition; that is, not only were Jews persecuted but also converts. If the positions converts occupied on councils are taken into account it is difficult to explain why those boards would have sanctioned acts of repression that necessarily affected converts. Second, the Catholic monarchs controlled council members.

In the main cities the presence of magistrates, royal nominees, prevented municipalities from becoming involved in certain tasks that were the privileged domain of the crown. These magistrates went to great lengths to avoid having persons designated as members of parliament who could lead any kind of opposition. The magistrates also obtained that those members of parliament would have limited conditional powers delegated by the crown. All this was orchestrated in such a way as to prevent all opposition from arising and in order to give free reign to the crown at all times. Under these conditions we must ask how urban oligarchies would have been able to impose as transcendent a decision as the expulsion of Jews on a regime as authoritarian as that of the Catholic monarchs. All in all, it seems highly unlikely.

In fact, none of these interpretations fits historical reality. They all attempt to uncover ulterior motives hidden behind ideologies for the edict of 1492. If instead of trying to discover what remains unspoken in the edict we attempt to analyze what is actually expressed in it, we discover a truism: The monarchs justified their decision on exclusively religious grounds. Primarily concerned with the total and definitive assimilation of converts, and given that previous measures had failed to achieve this, they had recourse to a drastic solution—expulsion of Jews to eradicate the evil at its source. Why not take this openly declared intention both literally and seriously? There is an antiheretical logic in the edict that should be not be overlooked. How can the purge against Jews and false converts be understood if we exclude inadequate explanations based on social and economic infrastructures?

Once the issue is posited in these clear terms we arrive at an admittedly sim-plistic response: The expulsion was motivated by the old Christians' hatred of Jews and converts, a revulsion the Catholic kings either shared personally or used in a demagogic manner to appease public opinion. In contemporary terms we might say that they were acquiescing to majority opinion. There is, however, nothing to suggest personal antipathy on their part. On the con-trary, everything indicates that the Catholic monarchs harbored no personal repugnancy for Jews and converts. Many of their closest collaborators were part of this group. Andrés de Cabrera, for example, exercised the decisive role in the proclamation of Queen Isabel, and Abraham Seneor was also active in the first months of the reign, lending money in times of penury. To him, the monarchs entrusted the financial mechanisms of the Holy Brotherhood, and he was also named major treasurer of the kingdom. We can think of many other Jews (e.g., Mayr Melamed and Isaac Abravanel) who occupied key posts, not forgetting the doctors who helped the queen in caring for her health or in delicate circumstances.[33] Brother Hernando de Talavera, Queen Isabel's con-fessor, was involved in all important events: the War of Succession, the com-plete reorganization of the Courts of Toledo, the establishment of the Holy Brotherhood, the War of Granada, and discussions with Columbus regarding the exploration voyages. The same was true of King Fernando's relations. The monarchs manifested no repugnance or personal hatred for Jews or converts. It is, moreover, difficult to understand how they continued to be surrounded by so many Jews and converts up until 1492 and so many converts after that date.

Would it be correct then to say that the monarchs were attempting to appease the masses by feigning to share prejudices that were not their own? That is more or less what Américo Castro suggests. The king—to whom Castro attributes the role of protagonist in this area—decided to expel the Jews in order to appease the people and create a popular monarchy.[34] That hypothesis makes no sense at all. The monarchs were imposing an authoritarian regime. They did not allow any of the *estamentos* (the noble states composing the Courts of Aragón) to be involved in political affairs. They tightly limited the privileges and jurisdiction of the clergy and reduced the role of the popular assembly. Why then would they have capitulated before public opinion, which at that time was neither well organized nor well represented? It is entirely improbable.

Elsewhere I have attempted to indicate which classes of society supported Fernando and Isabel's regime: basically, the nobility, the clergy, and the middle classes (cattle-raisers, merchants, and educated people). Indeed, the Catholic monarchs' political economy favored the *Mesta* (cattle and sheep owners involved in migratory cattle-raising and the export of merino wool and raw materials) to the detriment of farmers, artisans, and manufacturers, who were, in Pierre Vilar's terms, the "crushed classes." Although the majority of the population was composed of Castilian farmers, they constituted a silent majority whose interests were sacrificed because they had no voice in politics nor advocate to defend them.[35] Why would the Catholic monarchs have cared about the masses' opinions regarding Jews and converts when they did not bother to address the more basic concerns of those same masses?

Of the three versions of the expulsion edict—Torquemada's, the Castilian version, and the Aragonese version—only the third, signed by Fernando, referred to the theme of usury, albeit in very harsh terms.[36] In the other two versions there is not a single mention or the slightest allusion to that issue. Likewise, other accusations repeatedly made against Jews over the centuries were absent from the three versions of the edict—that is, Jews as a deicidal people, profaners of the host, or as guilty of ritual crimes.[37] The salient points of the decree refer to religious motives. There is not the slightest doubt that the repressive means used against Jews and converts were widely accepted by the old Christian masses. That does not mean, however, that those masses directly inspired such means.

Many contemporary scholars admit that religious zeal inspired the Catholic monarchs to expel the Jews at the time. It was not so much a matter of anti-Semitism in the modern sense of the word but rather anti-Judaism.[38] Based on these so-far correct assumptions, some go even further: Everything would be explained by the queen's fanaticism.[39] A devoted Catholic, she was ready to sacrifice everything to her faith in order to please God.[40] That argument is not very convincing. In short, it rings false. Fernando and Isabel were known as the Catholic monarchs (*Reyes Católicos*) after Pope Alexander VI conferred them with that title in 1494. At that time, the king of France was called the "Most Christian," giving the impression that he was somehow considered more Christian than other Western monarchs at the time. The decision of 1494 reestablished balance. The king and queen of Spain also merited special recognition for their fidelity to the faith and the Church. Moreover, in the case of Fernando and Isabel, who, strictly speaking, reigned only over Castile, León, Toledo, Aragon, and Valencia and as counts of Barcelona and elsewhere, the name was highly convenient. It avoided a long enumeration of kingdoms and territories. The title nevertheless has caused great confusion for those unfamiliar with the history of the period. Many take it too literally, believing that if Fernando and Isabel are called the Catholic monarchs, it must be for a very good reason. That is ridiculous if we seriously consider the pope who bestowed this title upon them. Alexander VI has not gone down in history as the beacon of evangelical virtue, Christian morals, and religious piety.[41] The confusion has nonetheless continued. Many still think of Fernando and Isabel as the Catholic monarchs because of that title and their politics as being inspired mainly by religious concerns: the reform of the clergy, the War of Granada, and—why not?—the creation of the Inquisition and the expulsion of the Jews. These last two events are completely consistent with the defense and exaltation of the faith.

I do not share this view. Fernando and Isabel were sincere Catholics and aimed at following the precepts and obligations that this supposed. It is possible that Isabel was even more religiously devout than Fernando and that she brought the cultivation of evangelical virtues to a level of perfection, which is why some have thought she should be canonized. I cannot (and do not) wish to comment on this subject, for it is a matter that Church scholars should decide. No one can be sure about the personal convictions of someone else. Historians can only try to examine facts objectively and competently. From that perspective Fernando and Isabel were monarchs and politicians whose conduct must be evaluated as such. Whatever their intimate feelings, their achievements can be appreciated in objective terms without appealing to religiously inspired motives. Before the beginning of their reign in 1473 Gómez Manrique, the poet and future collaborator of the crown, advised Princess Isabel: "They will not ask for an account of how you pray, nor how you are brought up; they will not question you about it. If you do justice, devoid of passion, if you punish the guilty or consent to evil-doers. . . . That will be the question" (No os demandarán/cuenta de lo que rezáis; / ni si os disciplináis / no os lo preguntarán. / De justicia si hicistes, / despojada de pasión; / si los culpados punistes, / o los malos consentistes. /. . . . Desto será la cuestión).

Manrique was, in essence, suggesting a political program to the future queen by advising her not to confuse the realm of religion with that of politics given their mutual incompatibility. Of course, the separation should not be taken any further. Fernando and Isabel were not indifferent to religious problems, nor could they be. Ultimately, Manrique was right. They were chiefs of state, and their main concerns were of a temporal nature; politics could not be second to religion. Machiavelli insinuated the opposite; for him, Fernando at least was tempted to use religion for political ends. All in all, the Inquisition was a political issue. The reestablishment of the monarchy's prestige, the creation of the modern state, the War of Granada, and the expansion in Italy and in the New World can all be explained without recourse to predominantly religious inspirations.[42]

There is no objective reason to tax the Catholic monarchs, or even Isabel alone, with religious fanaticism in the pejorative sense of the word. The expulsion of the Jews was a terribly harsh act implemented under especially inhumane conditions with no scruples or sense of respect. Yet this brutal inhumanity was not any worse than that of other events occurring in that era and in every era in Spain and elsewhere. Think of what happened during the War of Granada, for example, when the entire population of Málaga was reduced to slavery. Nothing would justify accusing the monarchs of religious fanaticism in their treatment of the Jews, as cruel as that treatment may seem. Reasons of state have often been cited to exonerate similar abuses of human rights.

There is no doubt that the idea of expelling the Jews originated with the Inquisition. Torquemada's provision, signed ten days before the monarchs' decree, was used as a template for the other edicts. For the Inquisition, expelling Jews appeared as the best way to resolve the problem of converts continuing to practice Judaism.[43] By eliminating its cause—communication with Jews—the crime would disappear.

These motives are broadly developed in the three versions of the expulsion edict. The Catholic monarchs adopted the idea, but that does not mean they did so under pressure from the inquisitors. Their preoccupations were also religious. They wanted to eliminate heresy and "cleanse" the kingdom of it as the queen had written. These preoccupations, however, were also political. They hoped that in eliminating Judaism they would ultimately facilitate the definitive assimilation and integration of converts into Spanish society. As Maurice Kriegel has written, the agreement between the inquisitors and the Catholic monarchs regarding the decision conceals underlying disagreement regarding the motives for that decision.[44]

I have cited on several occasions the correlation always present between periods of maximum anti-Jewish tension and economic crises or weakened political power, periods when Jews were accused of being responsible for difficulties or when factions used the Jewish theme to attract partisans to their cause. The murders of 1391 constitute the clearest demonstration of that rule. Hunger and penury coincided with a power void during which Fernán Martínez's energumens overstepped the bounds. The discriminatory measures enacted by the Catholic Monarchs, however, do not seem to match this pattern. Castile was undergoing a period of expansion, and there was no bold uprising against state power and its representatives. The Jewish community recovered, and royal power guaranteed its security. Nevertheless, this was precisely when Spanish Judaism was to suffer the gravest of tragedies in its history: total elimination.

Fernando and Isabel were advancing their monarchy in that period beyond medieval models. Something new was emerging that implied an original plan of execution. Luis Suárez Fernández is correct in situating the expulsion of the Jews as an integral part of the process of founding the modern state. That state was trying to impose authority—"royal absolute power"—on all groups and individuals in the kingdom and could therefore not be content with the heterogeneity of medieval times. It demanded greater social cohesion, and religious unity seemed to be the most appropriate means. "Before the nationalisms forged in the nineteenth century," wrote Braudel, "people did not truly feel linked by anything other than the sentiment of belonging to the same religion." Julián Marías explains this phenomenon very well: "In the progressively rationalist Modern Age, the principle of unitarianism and uniformity arose. It was believed that because Spain was Christian, the Spanish had to be Christians. The more or less clear notion elided into people thinking that he who was not Christian was not completely Spanish or was in some way 'disloyal,' an idea that just would not have occurred to a man during the Middle Ages."[45]

In the modern societies of Western Europe, when old regimes disappear the proprietorship of nations has been founded on standards other than religion: a common language, the same juridical norms, a common history, and values considered to be specific and shared by all citizens, all acting as the basis of patriotism. In societies of the Old Regime things were quite different. There was an identification of king, kingdom, territory, and society, and unity of religion founded the cohesion of the social body. That occurred throughout Europe in the sixteenth century, reinforced by the emergence of nation-states and the Protestant (Lutheran) Reformation.

The principle was thus posited that subjects had to be of the same religion as the prince, whether or not they liked it (*cujus regio ejus religio*). From the second half of the sixteenth century the principle was rigorously applied in Germany, in England, and, with certain nuances, in France.[46] For this reason, Protestants and Jews in France and Catholics in England were never considered true subjects of the king. Spain constituted no exception except that it surpassed the other nations, perhaps because it was not totally unified.

Beyond the differences that continued to exist among the Castilian territories and those of the Crown of Aragon, community of faith forged solidarity among subjects. The unique measures taken during the period from 1480 to 1492 signaled a significant change in the religious politics of medieval Spain and a singular case in the history of Christian Europe. With the end of the Reconquest the previously reigning medieval tolerance (or what was commonly referred to as such)—an accommodation made due to the peninsula's being divided between Moors and Christians—no longer made sense. Spain had been changed into one more Christian nation, just like the other Christian nations of Europe. It is no coincidence that the expulsion decree was signed three months after the fall of Granada.

Nevertheless, these circumstances only explain one aspect of the issue. There is another point that I think it opportune to highlight. What disappeared in 1492 was not only Judaism but also the Jewish community with its measure of relative autonomy. Some authors and essayists on this subject provide the impression that it was a matter of religious tolerance on an individual level. What could it have mattered to the sovereigns if some of their subjects were Jews and the majority Christians? In reality the situation before 1492 was much more complex. Judaism was not just an individual issue.[47] It was organized as a separate community, a microsociety on the fringes of a society formed by the Christian majority. Within the aljamas it was governed according to its own legal and cultural norms by its own leaders and judges. Not only were there places of worship for Jews but also schools, cemeteries, and other special structures. Agents for the aljamas met occasionally in assemblies to examine problems common to all, in particular but not exclusively contributions required by the crown. It was therefore true that Spanish Judaism was not a private and personal thing but rather a communitarian structure enjoying autonomy and constituting an enclave within feudal society, as Maurice Kriegel has noted.[48] Could a state, especially a modern state with its proclivity for rationalization, allow such a derogatory structure to stand separate from common law?

It is interesting to note that in contemporary republican, secular, and socialist France [1992] we have witnessed events that help us better comprehend the problem faced by the Catholic monarchs at the end of the fifteenth century. The presence of significant Muslim minorities seriously preoccupies authorities and has led to xenophobia and racism. Traditional French policy regarding immigration has always been to assimilate foreigners, to have them blend in with the rest of the population, notably by adopting the language and basic values of the new country. Where Italian, Spanish, Portuguese, and Polish immigrants were concerned, assimilation worked in a generally satisfactory manner because their cultural differences with the French were not so great. Not so with Muslims who try to maintain their collective identity and community not only in terms of religion but also with respect to their specific roots and cultural values such as Koranic law, polygamy, and the protection of women. Is the presence of such separate and autonomous communities compatible with the French nation's sense of ownership? This is the present debate: integration or insertion versus assimilation.[49]

We can observe certain curious coincidences with the way things unfolded in Spain in 1492.[50] One begins by affirming the right of each and every one to be different. Then a difference in rights is demanded, and that leads to the constitution of separate communities. I do not know if France will in the end be a multicultural nation. What is certain is that centuries went by in Spain before the Catholic monarchs resolved the issue in such a negative manner. The attempt to identify crypto-Jews and Jews meant that only Christians could be allowed to remain on Spanish soil. The monarchs must have thought that the prospect of expulsion would motivate a massive conversion of Jews to Christianity and that their progressive assimilation, through mixed marriages for the most part, would eventually eradicate the rest of Judaism. They were mistaken. Many Jews preferred to leave the country in spite of the discomfort, sacrifice, and abuse they suffered in order to keep their faith. The alternative of conversion and assimilation was roundly rejected.

If asked why similar treatment was not reserved for the Spanish Moors (*mudéjares*) who constituted a significant minority in the Valley of Ebro in the Kingdom of Valencia and in the recent conquest of Granada, I would respond that the difference in how Jews and Moors were treated in 1492 should not be interpreted as the sovereigns compromising in any way on establishing religious unity in Spain. Eliminating or assimilating the Moors seemed less urgent at the time. It was believed that the Moors would be converted gradually over time, also through mixed marriages. The first archbishop of Granada, Hernando de Talavera, developed an apostolate and a persuasive politics along those lines that contrasted with the violent methods used to convince Jews.

Because such politics were not likely to lead to immediate results, however, at the end of the fifteenth century authorities decided to cancel various guarantees granted to the Moors in 1492. This change in attitude provoked an uprising of the Moorish population of Granada in 1500. Two years later the Catholic monarchs applied similar discriminatory measures against the Moors. Like the Jews before them, they were obliged to convert to Catholicism or leave Spain. The majority preferred to remain in Spain and became Catholics, that is, new Christians. These Moorish Christians (*Moriscos*), in fact, changed little in their beliefs, ways of life, and customs. At the beginning of the seventeenth century they, too, were finally expelled from Spain.

In essence, the problem is the same, but the mudéjares and later the moriscos were very different from Jews and converts. They became downtrodden minorities closely kept in check by lords who exploited them as cheap and docile manual laborers. In particular, Moriscos—on the whole, new Christians like the Jewish converts—did not occupy high-ranking positions in society, administration, the clergy, or in business or commerce. They lived in the countryside (the *sierra*), were busy with their work, and generally did not become involved in Christian affairs. Accordingly, the authorities and the Inquisition were relatively patient and lenient for decades. That changed radically when Philip II came to power and decided to force them to renounce not only their beliefs but also their language, way of dress, and traditional customs. Just as with the Jews, a concerted effort was made to have the Moriscos assimilate into the rest of society, and once again the result was the same. Spain failed.

Epilogue

The expulsion edict of 1492 was not the last episode in the tragic history of Spanish Judaism. The majority of Jewish converts who maintained the right to remain in their country ended up blending into Hispanic society but were subjected to the Inquisition's vigilance fed by denunciations, both spontaneous and otherwise, made by members of the old Christian masses who continued to regard conversos as the sworn enemies of Roman Catholicism. Converts also suffer from discrimination as dictated by various institutions (colleges, confraternities, cathedral chapters, and religious and military orders) operating according to the concept of cleanliness of blood. Some converts remained faithful to the Jewish religion in secret in spite of the danger this entailed in inquisitorial Spain.

It would be beyond the scope of this book to outline, even in general terms, the history of peninsular crypto-Judaism. This history has had its dramatic episodes, for example the case of the Mallorcan Jews discovered at the end of the seventeenth century who had managed to practice their religion in secret for almost two hundred years. This was the origin of the *chuetas* (Balearic Island descendants of converted Jews) who suffered the social effects of rigorous discrimination until the beginning of the twentieth century. For other *Marranos,* who left by fleeing abroad, there are eighteenth-century records citing Spanish and Portuguese converts who appeared at synagogues just over the border in Bayonne or Bourdeaux, asked for circumcisions, and exchanged their Spanish names for others of Hebrew consonance.

Those circumstances and the loss of the influence of Spain contributed to the repulsion that surrounded the Inquisition and the expulsion of 1492. This had not been true at the beginning. Generally speaking, the expulsion was well received in Castile and in Europe. The University of Paris congratulated

Spain for having performed an act of good government, an opinion widely shared by some of the best minds of the period (e.g., Machiavelli, Guicciardini, and Pico della Mirandola) as emphasized by Antonio Domínguez Ortiz.[1] A measure that we now rightly judge as barbaric and inhumane appeared at the time to be quite natural and logical. So-called medieval *convivencia* had estranged Spain from Christian Europe. By allowing religious minorities to live, work, and freely practice their religions, had Al-Andalus and Christian Spain given proof of tolerance?

Before asking if such a thing were possible it would be useful to know what was at issue here. Religious freedom is a recent phenomenon, a conquest won from history. The battle to acquire it only began much later on with the victories the Enlightenment brought in this area. That said, much time went by before the affirmation of the rights of truth was supplanted by the affirmation of the right to err. Even today this does not necessarily convince everyone. I believe that it would be illusory to speak of medieval Spain as being ten centuries ahead of the evolution of the rest of the world.

Between the eighth and fifteenth centuries in the Iberian Peninsula, Christians and Muslims were convinced that they possessed the truth and that their religious creed was incompatible with others. If both groups have given the impression of being tolerant it is because they had no other choice. To tolerate, in effect, is to allow what cannot be prohibited, to be magnanimous when confronted with situations that cannot be helped. Muslim conquerors in the eighth century tolerated both Jews and Christians (those that were to form the *mozárabe* minority) because they were unable to convert or exterminate them. In the Christian kingdoms it was only after the great advances of the Reconquest during the twelfth century that Jews escaping the Almohads' fanaticism were welcomed and that Moors could remain in the recovered territories.

Thus the so-called *mudéjar* problem arose, that is, the presence of Moors who continued to be Muslim but were subjects of a Christian power. The way this problem was resolved had nothing idealistic to it. Due to a lack of laborers in the cities and countryside it was vital for Christians to retain mudéjares. As for Jews, they had become indispensable for their experience and knowledge of Arabic. Similar difficulties inspired the politics of the rulers of Aragon. When Alfonso el Batallador entered Zaragoza in 1118 he attempted to prevent the flight of Moorish peasants by all available means. This was the origin of Aragonese *mudejarismo,* not an ideology of tolerance and respect for others but rather a juridical answer to fulfill basic needs under specific circumstances.

A similar situation resurfaced a century later in Valencia and Murcia. In both areas the Aragonese monarchs had no other alternative. In order to cultivate the land it was essential for Moors to stay on and become mudéjares. It was also essential to avoid a depletion of manual laborers that would have catastrophic consequences. It was not the spirit of tolerance that allowed for the presence of *mozárabes* communities in Islamic lands (minorities of mudéjares in Christian kingdoms and Jews in all areas) but rather economic necessity. Américo Castro admitted this in the principle he devised in 1940 and 1941: "That the three religions coexisted is due less to tolerance than to vital weakness."[2]

Without a doubt the means the Catholic monarchs used constituted a break with the past. They put an end to a unique phenomenon in Christian Europe, a nation consenting to the presence of distinct religious communities. Historical circumstances had justified that peculiarity, but with the end of the Reconquest those circumstances changed. The tolerance of the previous era had lost its justification. In 1492, the same year in which Catholic monarchs invaded Granada, they expelled the Jews. I would not say that Spain then inaugurated an era of intolerance but that it was becoming a nation like others in Christian Europe. Perhaps that was unfortunate. Perhaps it would have been preferable for Spain to become a bridge or link between East and West. The historian can only comment on what actually happened. Obviously, the sovereigns of the period had nothing like that in mind. They wanted to assimilate conquered people and minorities by forcing them into conversions. They must have assumed that the task would have been much easier than it was. This mistaken impression reminds us of the phrase attributed to Fernando the Catholic in 1502 at the time of the forced conversion of the mudéjares of the Alpujarras when he said that these people would never be Christians but their children or grandchildren certainly would be. Did the Spanish monarchs give proof of intolerance in this instance? Undoubtedly, but no other European country of the period demonstrated what we could call tolerance. Sadly, in this case as in others Spain did not constitute an exception or separate case.

Starting in the sixteenth century all Europe rejected the idea that religious beliefs could be independent from nationality. After the Lutheran Reformation and the failure to reestablish the religious unity of Christianity, the principle of *cujus regio ejus religio* triumphed at the Peace of Augsburg (1530) and was confirmed by the Treaty of Westphalia (1548): The religion of each state would be decided by its rulers. The Germanic empire thereby disintegrated into a confederation of territories. In each, subjects had to profess the faith of their sovereign. The same occurred in England. In France guarantees were given to the Protestant Huguenots in accordance with the Edict of Nantes (1598) in the beginning, allowing them to hold onto their beliefs so long as these did not constitute political dissidence. Louis XIV, however, revoked the edict in 1685 and expelled the Protestants.

Despite that dramatic gesture, France was only complying with European legislation. In this case as in sixteenth-century Spain, events ran a parallel course. At first it was hoped that the Huguenots would gradually be assimilated by converting to Catholicism. Then it was thought that various types of pressures would accelerate the process. Finally, it was believed that threats of expulsion would finally convince those who hesitated in making the decisive move to convert.

Nonetheless, French Protestants did not convert en mass to Catholicism. Like so many Spanish Jews in 1492 they chose exile. The Catholic monarchs had rejoiced at the elimination of Spanish Judaism, and the French minister Louvois, responsible for the expulsion of the Protestants in 1685, was similarly elated to see the kingdom "purged" of dissident elements. Some of France's most brilliant writers (e.g., the Marquise of Sévigné, La Fontaine, La Bruyère, and even free-thinkers such as Fontenelle) also applauded the measure.[3]

Early modern Europe was still not able to accept the idea of the neutrality of the state with regard to different religious beliefs. Although such opinions began to be expressed, they fell on deaf ears for a very long time. In *De los nombres de Cristo* (1585) Brother Luis de León dedicated some magnificent pages against intolerance, fanaticism, and the admixture of politics and religion: "A kingdom is most ennobled . . . where no subject is considered vile due to his lineage nor insulted by the condition of being less well born than another. And it seems to me that this is how a true and honorable king should act: he should not allow any of his subjects to be considered vile or insulted [as a result of their birth]." Some thirty years earlier the anonymous author of *Viaje de Turquía* praised freedom of religion as it existed in Turkey:

> Suppose. . . . Turkey is not called Turkey because all of its people are Turks, because there are more Christians there who that practice their faith than there are Turks, although they are neither subjects of the Pope nor of our Latin church but have their own patriarch who they consider as their pope.
> Then why does the Turk consent to them?
> What does it matter to him, as long as they pay him his tribute, if they are Jewish or Christian or Moslem? In Spain, weren't there once Moors and Jews?

I see in this last phrase not so much a nostalgia for the Spain of the three religions as a first inkling of a modern idea, separation between Church and state, the idea that the state should be secular in character and religion has no reason to become involved in political matters. Identical conclusions can be found for the same date in the writing of the Valencian humanist Fadrique Furió Ceriol: "All good people, whether they be Jews, Moslems, Gentiles, Christians or of any other sect, belong to the same land, the same house and blood, and even all evil people are likewise the same."

Epilogue

Many years went by before that idea found favor. It took France until 1787 to grant legal existence to Protestants, and Jews had to wait until the Revolution of 1789 to be considered equal citizens. England took forty more years to recognize the civil rights of Catholics. And even now, can we really say that the religious neutrality of the state has been definitively imposed throughout the world? I would not dare pretend that this is true.

Appendix
The Expulsion Edicts

Decree for the Bishopric of Gerona from the Inquisitor General Torquemada, March 20, 1492[1]

Illustrious Lord Don Enrique, Infante of Aragon and Viceroy of the Principality of Catalonia by Our Lord and King.[2]

I, Friar Tomás de Torracremada of the Order of Preachers, prior of the Monastery of Santa Cruz of Segovia, confessor and advisor to the king and queen, our lords, and inquisitor general of heretical depravity[3] in all their kingdoms and dominions given and represented by the Holy Apostolic See, notify and inform Your Illustrious Lordship and the very Reverend Sir Bishop of Gerona and his general vicars and officials and the other ecclesiastical judges and the general governor's lieutenant[4] of the said principality and the bailiff, magistrate, council members, jurymen, aldermen,[5] constables and any and all other officials and their delegates and any and all squires, good men of the aforementioned city and bishopric of Gerona and the other towns and places in it and any and all persons, both clergy and laymen, of whatever state or condition they may be, and to each and every one of these to whom my letter is shown and comes to be known, that to the Inquisition that has taken place and is taking place in these kingdoms and in this bishopric, it has appeared and been demonstrated in trials and acts that great damage has befallen Christians as a result of the communing, conversation and communication that Jews have had [with them].[6] It has been proven that they have [through various] means, ways and manners [attempted?] to steal away [Christians] from our Holy Catholic faith and have them depart from it, bringing them and perverting them to their damned beliefs and opinions, instructing them in ceremonies and in observance of their law, making congregations[7] where they were read to and taught what they had to hold and keep and maintain in observance of the said law, arranging for circumcisions for them and for their sons, giving them books in which there were prayers to be made each year, and accompanying them in the temples of their ancestors in order to read and teach them the history of their law, informing them in advance of the festival of Passover, holidays, and mourning days, advising them of what they had to observe and do, giving them and placing unleavened bread in their hands and meat killed according to their ceremonies in order to celebrate these holidays and festivals, instructing them in things in which they had to partake, such as food and other things, convincing them as much as they could that they had to uphold and keep their law, making them understand that the Christians' law was a mockery and the Christians idolaters. All of this was rendered evident and attested to by a great number of witnesses and confessions, by both Jews and those they had perverted and tricked, thus resulting in great damage, detriment and infamy to our Holy Catholic faith, according to what has been made public and is known to all in these kingdoms and this bishopric.

And because it would be well to remedy [this situation and prevent] such great infamy [from continuing] to pay and offend the Catholic religion and there being no call to offend it any further, both those in God's good graces and those who have fallen and made amends and taken to an ordered life before our Holy Mother Church who, knowing and confessing their errors, have made penance; for them, there is no reason to return to relapse into vice, which, due to human frailty and science and diabolical suggestion that . . . makes war easily and rapidly[8] could, ... if the main cause were not removed. . . .the communing and communication that the. . . .Jews have until now had [with them] and . . . given this and documentation of the same, I agreed to notify our Lords the King and Queen and let them know of it.

And in accordance with the wishes of Their Highnesses, as Catholic Princes, [who have] agreed to decree in this matter, they have acted so that I may fulfill my role in the following way.

Thus, by the will and consent of Their Highnesses, I agree to give this letter of mine, in compliance with which I order any and all Jews and Jewesses, of whatever age they might be, from the aforementioned city and bishopric of Gerona and from all its towns and places and to each and every one of them, such that by the end of the first month of July [next July] of the present year, that they leave and absent themselves and depart from the said city and from everywhere in its bishopric and towns and places within it with all their sons and daughters, family members, male and female servants, and that they never return or enter, forever after, into any part of it, informing them that if they do not do this and comply with it and are found in the aforementioned city and bishopric or within its borders, that I will proceed and will order against them according to the law.

And so that this can be better accomplished and executed, I exhort and plead Your Very Illustrious Lordship and very Reverend Sir Bishop and your general vicars and officials and whatever other ecclesiastical judges and, under penalty of excommunication, I order the obedience of the aforementioned judges and secular officials and their delegates and any and all squires, good men of the aforementioned city of Gerona and the other towns and places of this bishopric, and any and all persons, whether clergy or laymen, in whatever state or condition. . . . and to each and every one of. . . . , upholding and complying with everything [contain]ed in this letter of mine and each thing in it and part of it.

And if the said Jews or any one of them do not [do so] to comply with what I have ordered by the deadline mentioned above and [instead] rebel against and disobey my orders, for a period of nine days following the deadline I hereby assign,[9] for which I give them three canonical admonitions and a peremptory [final, absolute] deadline, [thus] giving them three days for each deadline extension, you are not to participate or communicate in public or in private with said Jews or Jewesses or have or receive any of them in your places or houses nor offer them favors nor give or make them provisions or any victuals for their sustenance nor attempt to buy for them, purchase, trade or exchange or do any other things and that you are to separate them from your commerce and participation in all things, and now, not at any time nor in any manner, may you consent, allow or receive any of the aforementioned Jews or Jewesses, neighbors of the said city of Gerona and its bishopric and in all of its towns and places nor in any other parts, may they dwell or come or stay in this city or in any of the bishopric.

In thus doing and in so complying, you will do what you must in service of our Lord and in the glorification of our Holy Catholic Faith.

Conversely, once the deadline is past, given the same canonical admonitions, from this time forward, as set forth herein, We impose and promulgate the sentence of major excommunication against any and all of you who would do the contrary or would write the contrary or use such writings, the absolution of which I reserve for myself. Under the aforementioned penalty and sentence of excommunication, I order the said judges and secular officials of the said city and bishopric to make public and publicly proclaim this letter of mine in public places of this city and in the towns and places of this bishopric, each as it may be. . . . required and require the scribes to swear to read and faithfully make public the same. . . . and in authentic form.

And likewise, by virtue of obedience, all priests of all churches in the said city and bishopric that Sundays and holidays are to give sermons and make public for their parishioners how these Jews have to leave by a given time, and how after this time, they [Christians] may not communicate with them under penalty of excommunication.

In testimony of which We distribute and order distributed this letter of ours signed in our name and sealed with our seal, authenticated with our secret, issued in the city of Santa Fe, 20 days into the month of March, 1492, year of our Savior Jesus Christ.

By order of His Reverend Father; Johannes de Revenga.

Royal Decree from the King and Queen for the Kingdom of Castile, March 31, 1492[10]

Don Fernando and Doña Isabella, by the grace of God king and queen of Castile, León, Aragon, Sicily, Granada, Toledo, Valencia, Galicia, Mallorca, Seville, Sardinia, Cordoba, Corsica, Murcia, Jaen, the Algarve, Algeciras, Gibraltar, and the Canary Islands, count and countess of Barcelona and lords of Vizcaya and Molina, duke and duchess of Atenas and Neopatria, count and countess of Rosellón and Sardinia, marquis and marquesa of Oristán and Gociano.

To Prince Don Juan, my very dear and beloved son, and to the infantes, prelates, dukes, earls, counts, masters of the orders, priors, rich men, commanders (of the orders of knighthood or prefects of religious houses), governors of castles and fortresses of our kingdoms and dominions and to the councilors, correctors, mayors, governors, shepherds, gentlemen, squires, officials and good men of the very noble and very loyal city of Burgos and other cities and towns and places in its bishopric, other archbishoprics, and bishoprics and dioceses of our kingdoms and dominions and to the Jews' aljamas of the aforementioned city of Burgos and all the aforementioned cities and towns and places of its bishopric and all other cities, towns and places of our said kingdoms and dominions and to all Jews and to each person among them, both men and women, of whatever age they may be, and to all other persons of whatever law, state, dignity, preeminence and condition they may be, to whom what is contained in this our letter may or might concern in any manner, good tidings and grace.

You know, or should know, that because We were informed that in these our kingdoms there were some bad Christians who judaized[11] and insulted our holy Catholic faith, which was very much caused by the communication of Jews with Christians,[12] the Cortes that We held in the city of Toledo, in the past year fourteen hundred and eighty, ordered the separation of the aforementioned Jews in all the cities, towns, and places of our kingdoms and dominions and gave them juderías [quarters] in separate places where they were to live, hoping that with their separation they would be cured.

And furthermore, We requested and ordered that the inquisition be conducted in our aforementioned kingdoms and dominions, which, as you know, is twelve years old and that that has been done and is being done and through which many guilty have been found, as is generally known, and as We are informed by the inquisitors and many other religious persons, clerics and laymen, who have noted the great damage it appears that Christians have incurred and continue to incur in communing, conversing, and communicating with Jews, proving that they continue to manage, in as many ways and manners that they can, to subvert and detract pious Christians from our Holy Catholic faith and separate them from it and attract them to and pervert them with their damned beliefs and opinions, instructing them in ceremonies and observances of their law, making congregations where they read to them and teach them what they have to believe and observe according to their law, arranging to circumcise them and their children, giving them books and prayers to recite and informing them of the fasting days on which they have to fast and joining them to read and teaching them the stories of their law, notifying them of Passover in advance [before the Christian Easter], informing them of what they have to observe and do, giving and bringing them unleavened bread and meat killed in ceremonies, instructing them in things they have to keep separate, such as concerns food and as with other things in order to observe their law and convincing them as much as they can to keep and observe the law of Moses and making them understand that no other law or truth exists besides that one, as stated in many confessions and declarations by these same

Jews as well as by those who were perverted and tricked by them, resulting in great damage, detriment and disgrace to our holy Catholic faith.

And as it happened that We were informed of this in many places from many sources before now and We know that the true remedy for all the damage done and problems caused lies in completely severing any communication between these Jews and Christians and expelling them from our kingdoms, We had thought it would have been satisfactory to [just] send them out of all cities, towns and places in Andalusia, where it appeared they had done the most damage, believing that that would be enough for them to cease doing and committing the aforementioned in other cities, towns and places in our kingdoms and dominions.

And because We are informed that neither that nor the justice that has been done with regard to some of those Jews found to be very guilty of the said crimes and transgressions against our Holy Catholic faith were enough to obviate completely and remedy matters in such a way that such disgrace cease to offend the Christian faith and religion, for it is found and it appears that every day those Jews continuing their evil and damned propositions where they live and converse grow in numbers and because there is no reason to offend our holy faith any more, that those who until now the will of God has protected as fallen ones, who amended themselves and converted to the Holy Mother Church, against which due to human frailty and [through] tricks and diabolical suggestion they continue to wage war lightly, it has come to pass that the main cause of this has to be eliminated, that is, by expelling the said Jews from our kingdoms. Because when a serious and detestable crime is committed by some members of a college or university,[13] it is right that that college and university be dissolved and annihilated and the minors with the majors, and that some be punished for others and that those who pervert the good and honest living of cities and towns by contagion can damn others to be expelled from these towns, and some for others remove the cause of what damages the republic, even for the greatest and most dangerous and contagious of crimes, as is this one.[14]

Therefore, on the counsel and advice of some prelates and great men and gentlemen of our kingdoms and other persons of science and conscience in our Counsel, having much deliberated the matter, We agree to order the departure of all said Jews and Jewesses from our kingdoms and that they never return or come back to any one of them.

And moreover We order that this our letter be distributed by which We order all Jews and Jewesses, of whatever age they may be, whether living or residing or located in our said kingdoms and dominions, both natives and non-natives within them who, in whatever manner and for whatever cause, have come to be in them, that by the end of July of this year, they leave all of our stated kingdoms and dominions with their sons and daughters and male servants and maids and all Jewish familiars, both great and small, regardless of age, and that they dare not return to them, nor dwell in them or any part of them, living on or passing through them or in any other way, under penalty that if they do not do so and comply with this [order] and are found to be in the aforementioned kingdoms and dominions or come to them in any way, they will incur the death penalty and the confiscation of all of their household and financial belongings for the exchequer and treasury, punishments which they incur for so doing, without any other [right to] trial, sentence or declaration. We order that beyond the stated deadline of the end of July and henceforth and forever after, no person of our said kingdoms of whatever state, condition, or dignity they may be, is allowed to dare receive, abet, shelter, defend or keep publicly or secretly any Jew or Jewess, in their houses or in any other part of our said kingdoms and dominions, under penalty of losing all their possessions, vassals and fortresses and other inheritance and furthermore, of losing whatever mercy We have for our exchequer and treasury.

And because the aforementioned Jews and Jewesses may during the said time period until the end of the said month of July avail themselves of their persons and possessions and properties as they please, by this letter We take and receive them under our security and protection and royal defense, and We insure them and their possessions so that during the said time period until the said day at the end of the said month of July they can move [around] and be secure and can enter and sell and trade and transfer their belongings, furniture and landed properties, and dispose of them freely and that during the said time period no harm or damage or injustice of any kind be done to their persons or to their possessions against the law, under the penalties that those who violate our royal security are liable to and do incur.

And likewise, We allow and enable those said Jews and Jewesses to take their possessions and belongings out of all of our said kingdoms and dominions by land and by sea, as long as they do not take out either gold or silver or minted money nor other things prohibited by the laws of our kingdoms, except as merchandise and they not have prohibited items, even through exchanges. And moreover, We order all the councilors, judges, correctors, gentlemen, squires, officials and good men of the said city of Burgos and those of the other cities and places of our kingdoms and dominions and all our vassals, natural subjects to uphold and comply with this our letter and everything contained within it, and give it their full support and assist [matters] as much as necessary to do everything required by it, under penalty of our mercy and the confiscation of all their possessions and offices for our exchequer and treasury.

And because this [letter] comes to notify one and all and that no one can feign ignorance of it, We hereby order that this our letter be read aloud in the squares and usual places of this said city and in all the main cities, towns and places of its bishopric by the town crier and before the public scribe.

And that no one act or have enacted anything in any way [against this declaration] under penalty of our mercy and the stripping of any offices and confiscation of all belongings of anyone who would not comply.

And furthermore We order the man to whom We have sent our letter to appear before Us in our Court, in which We may be, from the summoning day until fifteen days following our said penalty, under which We order to whatever public scribe who for this [purpose] comes to be called to thereby give signed witness with his signature so that We know how our order has been carried out.

Issued in this Our city of Granada, the 31st day of the month of March, year of our Lord Jesus Christ, one thousand four hundred and ninety two. I the King. I the Queen.

I, Juan de Coloma, secretary of the King and Queen, our Lords, have written as ordered. Recorded by: Cabrera, Almazán, chancellor.

Royal Decree by King Don Fernando for the Kingdom of Aragon, March 31, 1492[15]

We, Don Fernando [...] to the very illustrious Prince Don Juan, our very dear and very beloved first son and universal successor to our kingdoms and lands, good health and paternal blessings, and to our general lieutenants, archbishops, bishops and whatever other prelates and to the dukes, marquis, counts and viscounts and to the governors, judges, bailiffs, [merino] wool traders and whatever other officials of our kingdoms, dominions, and cities, towns and places, each and every one of them, be they major or minor, and to the aforementioned cities, towns and places and to the councils of these and those and to all and whatever subjects and natives of ours, of whatever state, grade, gender, dignity and condition they might be, affectionate greetings, and to each and every one of the Jews' aljamas and to any Jews, men or women, however long they have been established in our kingdoms and dominions, whether they be or inhabit hither shore or thither shore, we notify and have you know as we are informed by the inquisitorial fathers of heresy and apostasy in the dioceses of our given kingdoms and established dominions, that many different Christians[16] have adopted Jewish rites and are living according to Jewish law and superstition, practicing their ceremonies and observing [Judaism] to the point of returning to abominable circumcisions, committing blasphemy against the holy name of Jesus Christ Our Lord and Redeemer, departing from the evangelical doctrine and His Very Holy Law and of the true cult of it, and that the said heresy and apostasy have had as their cause Jews and Jewesses dwelling and residing in our aforementioned kingdoms and dominions who, as we had feared, through conversation and communication they have had and have with the aforementioned Christians, intentionally and with great care and solicitude, induced and attracted them to this law of Moses, dogmatizing and teaching them the precepts and ceremonies connected to it. Thus, they made them observe the Sabbath on Saturdays and the [Jewish] Passover and other [Jewish] holidays, for which the aforementioned inquisitorial fathers in some of our cities and on some of our lands, by our will and with our permission, expelled the Jews and Jewesses who were in them, surmising that Christians who would separately judaize despite being informed about and accustomed to the holy Catholic faith, could in no way be cured. Convinced that the venerable father, prior of Santa Cruz, general inquisitor of the aforementioned heretical depravity in our kingdoms and dominions, in exercising his office and our royal conscience to eradicate completely this heresy and apostasy from all our kingdoms and dominions, would rid us of these Jews and Jewesses in perpetuity and forever after, saying that as a leper is as contagious as leprosy, no other remedy was possible besides this expulsion, and that he, given the responsibility he had, acted most appropriately in doing so, in making this request for our consent and favor, We decree and order the same. We, who chiefly desire that in our time the holy Catholic faith be prosperous and exalted and that heretical depravity in our kingdoms and dominions be completely eradicated, with mature and carefully considered deliberation in our sacred royal council, received additional information of these Jews' diabolical and disloyal persuasion and suggestions, of which our royal conscience is truthfully informed and certain, we find the nature and condition of the Jews for their feigned ignorance and great obstinacy in intentionally soliciting and [acting] so audaciously as to subvert Christians and very cautiously and astutely in bringing to their Jewish perfidy those who, for the most part, had come from [their fold and] were reputed to be more easily perverted.

And as the Jews for their own fault are subjected to perpetual servitude and are our servants and captives and if they are supported and tolerated it is by our piety and grace and if they fail to remember it and are ungrateful, not living pacifically and in the above-mentioned manner, it is a very just thing that they lose this grace of ours without which they are to be treated by us as heretics and purveyors of the aforementioned heresy and apostasy, by which [when] a crime is committed by some of a given college or university,[17] it is right that such a university or college be dissolved and annihilated and the minors along with the majors and some punished for others.

And, moreover, in addition to their immoderate and perverse way of life, we find these Jews to have devoured and absorbed Christians' properties and belongings, exercising iniquitously and pitilessly usurious depravity against the aforementioned Christians in public and acting as against enemies, claiming them to be idolatrous, [giving rise to] serious quarrels among our subjects and natives that have come to our attention and, as it was wished, we are resolving [these matters] we have come to know with the utmost diligence, since these Jews could not resolve [them] amongst themselves.

And given their perfidy and the very abominable and detestable acts committed by them, of which it is certain that by their obstinate infidelity they are incorrigible, it was therefore legitimate and permissible for us to punish them with more serious and greater punishments, yet we have decided to give them only such a punishment that, although it is less than what they deserve, we repute to be complete, since it gratifies the health of Christian souls, our subjects and natives, and their preservation and because their health requires their being separated from communing, conversation and communication with Jews and Jewesses, which has always in the past, in small and great ways, caused the aforementioned heresy and apostasy and the deterioration of Christians' possessions.

Mindful of the fact that Christians who have come to a land, to be manifest usurers and those who pervert chaste and honest living must be expelled from the cities and towns, just as those who by contagion can damage others and even for other slighter causes, although it concerns but political and public temporal utility, even more the usurious infidels, manifest seducers of Catholics and abetters of heresies between Catholic Christians, for the preservation and conservation of their souls and the Christian religion, must be expelled and separated, since removing the opportunity to err is to remove the error, and mindful of the fact that all bodies and all Jews who reside in our kingdoms and dominions are ours, to whom we can by our royal power and supreme jurisdiction order and avail to our will, using these for this very urgent and necessary cause, finally, aligning ourselves with the aforementioned prior father inquisitor general, supporting the Holy Office of this Inquisition whose authority in a Catholic manner relies on our will and consent accorded to the aforementioned father, by his letters, oversees the said general expulsion in support of the faith and for the great benefit of the spirits, bodies and possessions of our Christian subjects, for this our royal edict is forever after binding, we order expelling and we expel from all our Western and Eastern kingdoms and dominions all aforementioned Jews and Jewesses, great and small, who are and are found in our kingdoms and dominions, as in the sovereign (unappropriated) territories such as those of the Church and in others of whatever subjects and natives of ours and in whatever others contained within our kingdoms and dominions, from which Jews and Jewesses have to and must be obliged to leave and that they leave all of our aforementioned kingdoms and dominions between now and the end of the upcoming month of July, in such a way that past the said time any Jew or Jewess, great or small, of whatever age, cannot be or stay in any area of these our kingdoms and dominions, nor can they be able to return to them to stay or pass through them or through any part of them under penalty of death and the loss of [their] belongings to our exchequer and treasury, which penalty is to be incurred ipso facto and without trial or any declaration.

This same penalty is to be incurred by any persons of any preeminence or dignity or of any state or condition they might be who, after the stated time period, welcomes, keeps or receives any Jew or Jewess of any age in our aforementioned kingdoms and dominions or in any part of them, for those who would do such a thing [thereby] commit the crime of receiving and abetting heretics.

However, during the time period of forty days after the departure of these Jews and Jewesses, we will take the belongings of these [men and women] under our protection and defense and under our royal security and safeguard, in such a way that no one dare do them any harm or damage, either to their persons or belongings and whoever would do such, will then incur the punishment of the cessation of our royal security.

Finally, to you, illustrious prince, our son, our intent we declare, to your abovementioned prelates and clerics we say, exhort and render responsible, and to you, aforementioned dukes, marquis, counts, viscounts, nobles, barons, officials, subjects and natives of ours, according to how it pertains or may pertain to each one of you, we order that this our edict and everything contained within it be observed and enacted, to observe and enact it you do royally and in fact, if any one of you would act one and all to do or consent to the opposite, directly or indirectly: clerics, if you wish to have our grace and [given] the other stated penalties, you will avoid our ire and indignation. Nevertheless, whatever laws, statute-laws, constitutions, practices and customs [are enacted in] these our kingdoms and dominions and in each one of them, [none] may include the content of this our edict, nor order or dispose the opposite of it, in order that the said edict in support of the faith be enacted and executed [exactly], in adherence to and in support of the Holy Office of the Inquisition by whose authority the said expulsion is decreed.

And mindful that the above-mentioned Jews' aljamas and individual ones of these and other Jews collectively and individually are owing to and obliged to Christians, we decree and order that of their sedentary and removable belongings, rights, titles and stocks or shares, is done what by another of our edicts of the same date as this one will be published is decreed, to the effect that their creditors be paid and that what remains is left to them and returned to them and that they can freely take with them according to the manner prescribed in our provision referred to here above.

And so that no one can allege ignorance of the above, we order that the contents of the present [edict] be recited aloud by the town crier in the customary places in the cities of our above-mentioned kingdoms and dominions.

In testimony of which we order that this be done, with our secret seal affixed on the back.

Issued in our city of Granada, the thirtieth day of the month of March, year of Our Lord, 1492.

I the King.

Notes

Note: The text that appears between brackets has been added by the translator.

Introduction

1. Américo Castro, *La realidad histórica de España* (Mexico City: Porrúa, 1962).

2. J. N. Hillgarth, *The Spanish Kingdoms, 1250–1516,* 2 vols. (New York: Oxford University Press, 1976).

3. David Nirenberg, *Communities of Violence: Persecution of Minorities in the Middle Ages* (Princeton: Princeton University Press, 1996).

4. William Chester Jordan, *The French Monarchy and the Jews. From Philip Augustus to the Last Capetians* (Philadelphia: University of Pennsylvania Press, 1989), pp. 200–238.

5. Manuel Colmeiro, *Cortes de los antiguos reinos de León y de Castilla* (Madrid: Real Academia de Historia/Rivadeneira, 1882), vol. 4, petition 11, pp. 67–68.

6. Colmeiro, *Cortes de los antiguos reinos,* vol. 4, petition 34, p. 101.

7. Ibid., petition 25, vol. 4, pp. 94–95.

8. Ibid., petition 36, vol. 4, pp. 102–4.

9. Ibid., petition 12, vol. 4, pp. 69–70.

10. An Israeli scholar, Yom Tov Assis, attributes this golden age to the relative freedom from persecution that Jews enjoyed in Muslim parts of Spain. He maintains that Jews were also able to remain an integral culture because under the Umayyad Muslims they could maintain contact with the Babylonian center of Judaism. Assis's paper, delivered at the Notre Dame Conference in Medieval Studies in 1994, is not included in the volume published from that event: *Christians, Muslims, and Jews in Medieval and Early Modern Spain: Interaction and Cultural Change,* edited by Mark D. Meyerson and Edward D. English (Notre Dame, Ind.: University of Notre Dame Press, 2000).

Preface

1. The reference was to a "spiritual and physical holocaust of the Jewish people."

2. John Edwards, *The Jews in Christian Europe, 1400–1600* (New York: Routledge,

1988), 12; Fernand Braudel, *La Méditerranée et le monde méditerranéen à l'époque de Phillippe II,* 2 vols. (Paris: Hachette, 1966), vol. 1, p. 380.

3. See the discussion opposing Karl Marx and the Lutheran theologian Bruno Bauer in 1843. The Jews attempted to emancipate themselves, demanding civil rights and religious freedom, both of which supposed a secular state, something that did not yet exist in Germany at the time. I have modified the spelling of the medieval texts for the benefit of modern readers.

Chapter 1: The Jews in Medieval Spain

1. The identification of Sephardic with Spain comes from a prophesy Abdías made alluding to the exiles of Jerusalem who were in *Sefarad,* that is, in the hinterlands of the Roman Empire, according to late interpretations. Yitzhak Baer, *Historia de los judíos en la España cristiana,* translated by Jose Luis Lacave, 2 vols. (Madrid: Altalena, 1981), vol. 1, p. 13. When did the term begin to designate the Jews established in Spain? The matter remains unclear. It is doubtful that the expression was in use during the Middle Ages. The most probable explanation is that the Biblical *Sefarad* and the Iberian peninsula were equated later on, some time after the expulsion of 1492.

2. [The verb *judaizar* is used throughout this volume and in the 15th century expulsion edicts. Occasionally, we translate simply as "practicing Judaism" or "practicing crypto-Judaism." Here, as is stated, it refers to Christians who practiced Judaism as a result of contact with Jews implicating that this was due to some form of Jewish proselytism.]

3. In approximately 420, a card written by Bishop Severo de Menorca mentions the persecution of prosperous, numerous, and influential Jews in Mahon. The synagogue was destroyed and the community converted to Christianity. See Luis García Iglesias, *Los judíos en la España antigua* (Madrid: Christiandad, 1978), pp. 87–89.

4. The Council definitively prohibited marriages of Christians with Jews, eating at the same table, and adultery committed between Christians and Jews.

5. *De fide catholica contra Judaeos, De nativitate Christi ex Isaiae testimoniis.*

6. The Fourth Council (in 633) "revived the old norm that there not be any contact between Jews and Jewish converts" (García Iglesias, *Los judios,* p. 112). As for Ervigio's legal statutes, the harshest ever dictated against the Jews, it was approved by the Twelfth Council, although it might have been an initiative of the ecclesiastical estates (ibid., p. 139).

7. The accusation runs throughout the Middle Ages and figures prominently in the Blood Purification Statute elaborated by Pero Sarmiento for the city of Toledo in 1449.

8. García Iglesias, *Los judíos,* pp. 200–201. [For a slight variation on this translation, see Ahmed ibn Muhammad Al-Makkari, *History of Mohammedan Dynasties in Spain,* translated by Pascual de Cayangos (London, 1840): "Whenever the Muslims conquered a town, it was left in the custody of the Jews, with only a few Muslims the rest of the army proceeding to new conquests; and where the Jews were deficient (in

numbers) a proportionately greater body of Muslims was left in charge" (pp. 280–82, see also p. 531n18, but cf. p. 511n15).]

9. Baer, *Historia de los judíos,* vol. 1, p. 19.

10. Ibid., p. 29.

11. [The same term can apply to assemblies of Muslims or Moors in mosques.]

12. [The *Reconquista* was the war that Christians waged to reoccupy lands previously conquered by Muslims in the Hispanic peninsula; it ended in 1492 with the fall of Granada.]

13. Ibid., pp. 90–91.

14. This family formed part of the initial clientele of the Knights of the Temple, from whence they took their name.

15. Baer, *Historia de los judíos,* vol. 1, pp. 118–19.

16. Ibid., vo. 1, p. 137.

17. Luis Suárez Fernández, *La expulsión de los judíos de España* (Madrid: Editorial MAPFRE, 1991), vol. 1, p. 111.

18. Luis Suárez Fernández, *Judíos españoles en la edad media* (Madrid: Rialp, D.L., 1980), pp. 96–98. This estimate is based on the well-known Huete tax list of 1391 that tallied 2,801,345 *maravedís* [Spanish coin currency] in contributions; thirty were required from each Jewish male more than twenty years of age, whether married or head of household.

19. Baer, *Historia de los judíos,* vol. 1, p. 154.

20. Suárez Fernández, *La expulsión de los judíos,* vol. 1, pp. 25–26.

21. Baer, *Historia de los judíos,* vol. 1, pp. 341–43.

22. Suárez Fernández, *La expulsión de los judíos,* vol. 1, p. 25.

23. Baer, *Historia de los judíos,* vol. 1, pp. 170, 243.

24. As early as in the *Cantar del Cid,* the Jew is portrayed as a crafty merchant and usurer.

25. Béatrice Leroy, *Une famille sépharad à travers les siècles: Les Menir (XII-XXe siècles)* (Paris: Editions du Centre national de la recherche scientifique, 1985).

26. Baer, *Historia de los judíos,* vol. 1, p. 243.

27. Ibid., vo. 1, pp. 33, 63.

28. J. M. Monsalvo Antón, *Teoría y evolución de un conflicto social: El antisemitismo en la Corona de Castilla en la Baja Edad Media* (Madrid: Siglo Veintiuno, 1985), p. 188.

29. Monsalvo Antón, *Teoría y evolución,* p. 164.

30. Ibid., p. 144.

31. The *Fuero de Cuenca* states: "If a Jew and a Christian contest something, they designate two neighboring townspeople, one Christian and one Jewish." In the *Fuero de Sepúlveda,* a Jew's testimony was considered as valid as a Christian's.

32. Baer, *Historia de los judíos,* vol. 1, p. 145.

33. Ibid., vol. 1, p. 178.

34. Ibid., vol. 1, pp. 136–37.

35. Ibid., vol. 1, p. 253.

36. Investigations made by Yom Tov Assis, professor at the University of Jerusalem, show this intermediary role of Catalonia and specify how it was via Catalonia that Judeo-Muslem culture made its way to the north.

37. Averroes (Ibn Rushd in Arabic), whom Dante called "the author of the great commentary," was born in Córdoba in 1126. A physician, theologian, and jurist in addition to philosopher, he became known through his commentaries on Aristotle's books. He read these books in Arabic translation, when Latin and Greek translations were unknown. In the name of science he attacked the religious opinions of the ignorant masses. As a precursor to rationalist tendencies in philosophy, his influence was immense among both Jews (Maimonides never cites him but was inspired by his commentaries) and Christians (Thomas knew of his work). Averroes still had influence in the sixteenth century (Pomponazzi, Vanini, and the School of Padova) and the seventeenth century among the first proponents of free thought.

38. "Sexual license was in large part nothing more than a phenomenon secondary to free thought and religious rationalism which brought national treason along with it." Baer, *Historia de los judíos,* vol, 1, p. 191.

39. Ibid., vol. 1, p. 192.

40. The case of a Jewess in Coca is known. Because she had slept with a Christian, the aljama ordered that her nose be cut off.

41. A copy of a book in Catalan is preserved at the El Escorial library, part of the personal collection of the Count-Duke of Olivares.

42. In the nineteenth century Jaime Luciano Balmés defined tolerance as it was practiced in the Middle Ages as "the suffering of something ill-conceived, but which was believed to be convenient to leave as such without punishment . . . in such a way that the idea of tolerance is always accompanied by the idea of a fault."

43. Gilbert Dahan's *Les intellectuels chrétiens et les Juifs au moyen âge* (Paris: Editions du Cerf, 1990) offers a good presentation of this issue.

44. "They should not be appointed to office or be given distinctions by kings or other titled princes whatsoever." In Pedro de Cuéllar's catechism of 1325 it was stated that the kings "sinned in appointing to office Jews over Christians."

45. Spanish Jews took pains on several occasions to show that their ancestors had no responsibility in the murder of Jesus Christ. In one of the versions of the *Crónica general de España,* written around 1450 and entitled *Refundicion de la crónica de 1344,* there are cards supposedly sent by Jews in Toledo to their brothers in Jerusalem begging them not to put Jesus of Nazareth to death. Baer, *Historia de los judíos,* vol. 2, p. 533.

46. Monsalvo Antón, *Teoría y evolución,* p. 215.

47. The first mention of such a thing occurred in Zaragoza in the middle of the thirteenth century. At the end of the century, in 1294, also in Zaragoza, the rumor was that the Jews had killed a Christian child and torn out his heart and liver. This time, however, Jews managed to track down the child, who was in perfect health, which led to the king's severe reprimand of the municipality. Baer, *Historia de los judíos,* vol. 1, p. 311. Three Jews were executed in Barcelona on this charge [profanation of the Host] in 1367.

Chapter 2: The Crisis in the Fourteenth Century

1. Persecutions and expulsions "are always dependent on the vagaries of economic life, they accompany them. . . . The major culprit is recession" [sont toujours sous la dépendence des intempéries de la vie économique, elles les accompagnent. . . . La culpabilité majeure est celle de la récession]. Fernand Braudel, *La Méditerranée et le monde méditerranéen à l'époque de Phillippe II,* 2 vols. (Paris: Hachette, 1966), vol. 2, p. 150. See also the commentary written as a postface by Max Horkheimer for Thilo Koch's *Porträts zur deutsch-jüdischen Geistesgeschichte* (Cologne: M. DuMont Schauberg, 1961): "[The Jews] had learned over the centuries how much Christian and Muslim tolerance was linked to a thriving economy. Wherever recession, misery and oppression occurred, the Jews were used to being the first victims." From the French translation in *Esprit* (May 1979): 23.

2. As King Fernando IV said after the conquest of Gibraltar, "To do well and mercifully for the council of Gibraltar, in order that he [the king] gain more riches and peoples . . . we order that all those Christians, Moors, or Jews, that traded victuals in Gibraltar be duty free and that they pay no rights on anything they may sell and that they sell what they can." J. M. Monsalvo Antón, *Teoría y evolución de un conflicto social: El antisemitismo en la Corona de Castilla en la Baja Edad Media* (Madrid: Siglo Veintiuno, 1985), p. 213.

3. Luis Suárez Fernández is certain in observing, "It's a general rule . . . the one that connects the general well-being of the Jews with periods of affirmation of royal power." Suárez Fernández, *Lu expulsión de los judíos de España* (Madrid: Editorial MAPFRE, 1991), vol. 1, p. 150.

4. Yitzhak Baer, *Historia de los judíos en la España cristiana,* translated by Jose Luis Lacave, 2 vols. (Madrid: Altalena, 1981).

5. José Luis Martín and Julio Valdeón Baruque among others.

6. Was it a matter of the maritime and commercial bourgeoisie being pitted against the land-owning nobility? That is the thesis Carmelo Viñas Mey has advocated for many years.

7. A judicial investigation took place in 1329 and confirmed responsibility of the city of Estella, which was condemned to pay a fine of 10,000 pounds into the Royal Treasury each year for a period of ten years.

8. Baer, *Historia de los judíos,* vol. 1, p. 328.

9. Ibid., vol. 2, p. 333.

10. William H. MacNeil, *Plagas y pueblos* (Madrid: Siglo Veintiuno Editores, 1984), p. 181. These assaults most likely led to the migration of Jews in significant numbers toward Eastern Europe and Poland in particular.

11. The following statement was found in documents in the South of France: "Puteos et acquas infecerant et aerem corrumperunt" (Monsalvo Antón, *Teoría y evolución,* p. 221).

12. Baer, *Historia de los judíos,* vol. 1, 318.

13. See the prologue by Ernest Labrousse to the French translation of the book by

R. H. Tawney, *La religion et l'essor du capitalisme* (Paris: Librarie M. Rivière et Cie, 1961), p. xi.

14. Moreover, it is well to note that the Talmud also prohibits usury. Jews could not lend money at interest to fellow Jews. Monsalvo Antón, *Teoría y evolución*, p. 63.

15. From this comes the name given to partisans of Pedro I, *emperejilados* or something like "Pedrolizers."

16. Julio Valedeón Baruque, *Los conflictos sociales en el Reino de Castilla en los siglos XIV y XV* (Madrid: Siglo Veintiuno, 1975), p. 131.

17. Baruque, *Los conflictos sociales,* pp. 134–35.

Chapter 3: The Convert Problem (1391–1474)

1. J. M. Monsalvo Antón, *Teoría y evolución de un conflicto social: El antisemitismo en la Corona de Castilla en la Baja Edad Media* (Madrid: Siglo Veintiuno, 1985).

2. Philippe Wolff, "The 1391 Pogrom in Spain: Social Crisis or Not?" *Past and Present,* 50 (Feb. 1971): 4–18.

3. Pierre Vilar, *La Catalogne dans l'Espagne moderne* (Paris: SEVPEN, 1962; [Barcelona: Catalunia en la España moderna, Crítica, 1977, 1987, and 1988]), vol. 1, p. 477.

4. Vilar, *La Catalogne,* p. 467.

5. The Council of One Hundred in Barcelona contracted security guards to protect the Jewish quarter but could not prevent the assault on August 5 and the murder of a hundred persons. The next day they ordered the hanging of ten of the aggressors, which provoked new confrontations with the cry "Visca lo rey e lo poble" and accused the authorities of protecting the Jews. Luis Suárez Fernández, *La expulsión de los judíos de España* (Madrid: Editorial MAPFRE, 1991), vol. 1, pp. 199–201.

6. Monsalvo Antón, *Teoría y evolución,* pp. 256–57. [These sentences have been rearranged in an attempt to better convey the sense intended.]

7. Suárez Fernández, *La expulsión de los judíos,* vol. 1, p. 188.

8. Béatrice Leroy, *Une famille sépharad à travers les siècles: Les Menir (XII-XXᶜ siècles)* (Paris: Editions de Centre national de la recherche scientifique, 1985), p. 64.

9. Yitzhak Baer, *Historia de los judíos en la España cristiana,* translated by Jose Luis Lacave, 2 vols. (Madrid: Altalena, 1981), vol. 2, pp. 377–78. Juan Sánchez de Calatayud was the grandfather of Gabriel Sánchez, one of the officials of the Catholic king.

10. Suárez Fernández, *La expulsión de los judíos,* vol. 1, p. 192.

11. Léon Poliakov, *Histoire de l'antisémitisme,* vol. 2: *De Mahomet aux Marranes* (Paris: Calmann-Lévy, 1961), pp. 160–61.

12. His son, Alonso de Cartagena (ca. 1385–1456) was later deacon of the Cathedral of Santiago in 1422.

13. Baer, *Historia de los judíos,* vol. 2, pp. 377–78.

14. Suárez Fernández, *La expulsión de los judíos,* vol. 1, pp. 210–12. Baer cites the case of a Mallorcan Jew, Mossé Faquim, who was a declared Averroist: "His own fellow Jews told the King about him in January 1391. Already very close to the time of the persecutions, he was denounced as having mocked all religions. . . . He drank Chris-

tians' wine and ate pig meat, did business on Saturday, attended the Christian court and paid money. . . . There were men of this sort in all the large Jewish communities of Spain." *Historia de los judíos,* vol. 2, pp. 346–47.

15. The apostolate of Saint Vicente Ferrer in Valladolid culminated in the winter of 1411–12 and ended with the incarceration of the Jews on January 2, 1412. In a work entitled *Silva palentina* written in the sixteenth century, Alonso Fernández of Madrid stated, "He was the cause of many thousands of conversions of infidels in Spain and especially . . . the baptism in Castile of twenty five thousand Jews and eight thousand Moors and most of the Jews who lived in this city of Palencia were then converted and baptized." The Bishop of Palencia—Alonso Fernández continues—was not pleased with this massive conversion because the Jews, as Jews, paid special taxes. To compensate the loss King Juan II ceded a third of his lands to the bishop.

16. Don Pedro de la Caballería was baptized in 1414. A famous jurist in his time, he was murdered in 1461 during a revolt of the Catalan people against Juan II. Despite his apology of Christianity, written in 1450 and entitled *Zelus Christi contra Judaeos, Sarracenos et infieles,* it appears that he was one of the fifteenth century's first crypto-Jews or false Jewish converts. *Criptojudíos* or *judaizantes* are terms referring to converts who secretly practiced Jewish rituals such as prayers and the observation of the Sabbath. All this was discovered much later on in 1480, when inquisitors investigated the practices of his descendants. Various testimonies revealed curious details of Don Pedro de la Caballería's crypto-Judaism showing that his conversion was an act of opportunism. To a modest Jewish tailor who was shocked that a man so well-versed in Judaism would convert to Christianity, Don Pedro de la Caballería responded, "Shut up, fool; what could I amount to, staying a Jew. . . . head rabbi? Now I have sworn my faith to the crucified [*el enforcadillo,* in reference to Jesus] and now they shower me with honors and I command and watch over the entire city of Zaragoza." Don Pedro added that before his conversion he never dared go out on a Saturday, but "now I do what I want," including eating during the fast of Yom Kippur if he felt like it. Baer, *Historia de los judíos,* vol. 2, pp. 528–29.

17. Baer writes that especially in Aragon, the rich and well-known Jews of the aljamas converted to Christianity, whereas those who remained faithful to Jewish tradition were more likely to have been artisans (and remain poor) or very devout men and Torah scholars (ibid., vol. 2, p. 492). A bit further on (pages 498–99), he quotes a Jewish author of the period: "The majority of the highway robbing tax collectors abandoned their religion rather than find themselves without rents and payments to collect since they had not learned any other way to make a living. So it was that when they were faced with ruination, penury and prison, some of the artisans also abandoned their religion when they saw these doings and adversities."

18. Poliakov, *Histoire de l'antisémitisme,* vol. 2, p. 169.

19. A fiscal census from Enrique IV's time shows how debilitated the Andalusian Jewish community was after the events of 1391. Jews paid 2,500 *maravedís* in Seville, 7,300 in Jerez de los Caballeros, 6,000 in Segura de la Orden, 3,500 in Llerena, and

2,000 in Moguer, while those of Segovia paid 11,000 and those of Avila 12,000. Claudio Guillén, "Un padrón de conversos sevillanos," *Bulletin Hispanique* 65 (1963): 52.

20. A list is given in Melquíades Andrés, *La teología española en el siglo XVI* (Madrid: 1976), vol. 1, pp. 310ss.

21. Baer, *Historia de los judíos*, vol. 2, p. 508.

22. Ibid., vol. 2, pp. 16, 194.

23. Ladero cites this passage from Pulgar: "In Andalusia, there are ten thousand young, unmarried girls between ten and twenty years old who from birth had never left their houses or known anything other than what [doctrine] they learned from their parents."

24. Francisco Márquez Villanueva, "Conversos y cargos concejiles en el siglo XV," *Revista de la Biblioteca, Museos y Archivos* 63 (1957): 503–40.

25. Ladero Quesada questions the amplitude of this phenomenon: "Where is this intense infiltration, the converts' so-called domination in the council-boards? It doesn't exist anywhere" (Miguel Ángel Ladero Quesada, "Europa en la historia," *Historia 16* no. 194 [1992]: 39–51). That is because Ladero was working with specific sources, lists of those sentenced by the Inquisition and those rehabilitated by paying compensation. Not all the converted aldermen (*regidores*) suffered from the rigors of the Inquisition.

26. Francisco Márquez Villanueva, introduction to Hernando de Talavera, *Católica impugnación* (Barcelona: Juan Flores, 1961), p. 49. In the same spirit we can cite the case of the convert from Aragon who used to say, "There is nothing more of a paradise than the Calatayud market."

27. After winning the rebellion Sarmiento abandoned the city of Toledo on December 17, 1449. With permission to take along his personal belongings, he packed the booty gained through pillaging and extortion. Almost two hundred beasts of burden were packed with loot from his excessive ventures in the form of gold, silver, tapestries, brocades, and cloth from Holland and Brittany that his followers sacked for him, as a journalist of the period related, "[in robberies mandated by Sarmiento where orders stated] that they should not leave the house they were sent to rob until nothing was left inside." The value of the goods exceeded 30 million *maravedís*. Victims' protestations were of no use; Sarmiento was able to keep his spoils. Eloy Benito Ruano, *Toledo*, 58–59.

28. M. A. Ladero Quesada reviews the principal works used for these polemics at the time in *Los Reyes Católicos: la corona y la unidad de España* (Madrid: Association Francisco Lopez de Gomara, 1979), pp. 214–15.

29. Nevertheless, a later bull, *Regis pacifici*, dated October 28, 1450, rectifies this attitude. Although it confirms the previous position from a theoretical point of view it considers that its immediate application could cause scandals, dissension, and various other problems. Tarsicio de Azcona, *Isabel la Católica* (Madrid: Biblioteca de Autores Cristianos, 1993), p. 377.

30. Antonio Domínguez Ortiz, *Los Judeoconversos en España y América* (Madrid: Ediciones Istmo, 1971), p. 31.

31. Ladero Quesada, *Los Reyes Católicos*, p. 211.

32. Baer, *Historia de los judíos*, vol. 2, p. 554. Similar phenomena occurred in the Kingdom of Aragon. Baer cites the case of several converts detained in Valencia in 1464 who intended to depart for Constantinople (p. 540).

Chapter 4: Jews and Converts in the Catholic Monarchs' Spain (1474–92)

1. Tarsicio de Azcona, *Isabel la Católica* (Madrid: Biblioteca de Autores Cristianos, 1993), p. 629.

2. Azcona, *Isabel*, p. 629.

3. Ibid., p. 630.

4. Luis Suárez Fernández gives a few examples such as that of the Valmaseda aljama destroyed in an attack. Royal justice sided with the Jews, but they did not dare return and preferred to content themselves with receiving an indemnity for damages. The Bilbao Council also circumvented and mocked the monarchs' orders. It had prohibited Jews from the Medina de Pomar to continue to buy cloth, silk, and linen, but on March 12, 1475, the monarchs declared the ban null and void. The Bilbao Council then prohibited Jews from circulating at night in town, which meant they had to stay in unsafe areas where there were robbers. It thus became impossible to conduct business.

5. Maurice Kriegel, "La prise d'une décision: l'expulsion des juifs d'Espagne en 1492," *Revue Historique* 240 (1978): 49–90, quotation on 49.

6. Luis Suárez Fernández, *Judíos españoles en la edad media* (Madrid: Rialp, D.L., 1980), p. 257.

7. The uprising in Segovia in 1477 cannot be strictly assimilated to previous anti-convert disturbances. It was motivated by the monarchs' gift of a large domain to the new Count of Chinchón, Andrés Cabrera, in recognition for his prior services to the crown. The creation of the domain meant the transfer of a part of the community district of the city, Segovian land. That was the reason for the rebellion in Segovia, which Doña Isabel was personally obliged to quell. The rioters apparently did not seriously exploit the fact that Cabrera was a convert.

8. The word already existed at the end of the fourteenth century. In the Courts of Soria (1380) we read the following: "whoever—Christian or Jew—calls someone marrano or *tornadizo* [turncoat] or uses other injurious words for those who turn away from the Catholic faith will pay a fine of 300 maravedís each time they use the term" (J. M. Monsalvo Antón, *Teoría y evolución de un conflicto social: El antisemitismo en la Corona de Castilla en la Baja Edad Media* [Madrid: Siglo Veintiuno, 1985], p. 251). Nevertheless, it seems that the term was widely used in the fifteenth century. The etymology is much debated, see David Gonzalo Maeso, "On the Etymology of the 'Marrano' Voice," *Sefarad* 15 (1955): 379–85.

9. "They had a presumption of haughtiness, such that no one in the world was better, finer, more astute or more honorable than they, due to their lineage descending from the tribes and land of Israel." Andrés Bernáldez, *Historia de los Reyes Catholicos*, 2 vols. (Seville: J. M. Geofrin, 1870).

10. From one of the small volumes that most contributed to spreading anti-Jewish propaganda, the *Libro del Alborayque,* comes the following: "Sodomy came from the Jews. . . . from the Jews, it was passed along to the Moors and then to Christian males, like Diego Arias" (King Enrique IV's accountant). The *Libros del Alborayque* was written in approximately 1488, and the text was published at the end of the last century by F. Fita in the *Boletín de la Real Academia de la Historia, XXIII* (1893), pp. 369–443. Nicolás López Martínez has studied and analyzed it in *Los judaizantes castellanos y la Inquisición en tiempo de Isabel la Católica* (Burgos: Aldecoa, 1954).

11. "A ti, fray Diego Arias, puto, / que eres y fuiste judío, / contigo no me disputo, / que tienes gran señorío; / águila, castillo y cruz, / dime de dónde te viene, / pues que tu pija capuz/nunca le tuvo ni tiene" [To you, brother Diego Arias, a whore / who is and was a Jew / I don't argue with you / for you have a large domain / an eagle, a castle and a cross / tell me from whence it comes to you / that your hooded pisser / never had it, nor do you have it now].

12. In approximately 1454 robbers killed a boy for the gold chain he was wearing around his neck. Brother Alonso de Espina was not satisfied with that version of the crime and explained in his sermons that Jews had murdered the boy and taken out his heart to eat it cooked in wine (Luis Suárez Fernández, *La expulsión de los judíos de España* [Madrid: Editorial MAPFRE, 1991], vol. 1, p. 253). It was rumored that during Holy Week in 1468 Jews from Sepúlveda crucified a child.

13. According to a landowner in 1491, there were 216 of them.

14. Fewer than 1,500 individuals continued living in the splendid old Jewish neighborhood that had become too large for their dwindling numbers and into which Christian families had moved.

15. With some three thousand people, a fourth or a fifth of the population, the Jewish community of Avila was one of the most populous in the kingdom. P. León Tello, "La judería de Avila durante el reinado de los Reyes Católicos," *Sefarad* 23 (1963): 36–53.

16. Yitzhak Baer, *Historia de los judíos en la España cristiana,* translated by Jose Luis Lacave, 2 vols. (Madrid: Altalena, 1981), vol. 2, p. 505. Baer adds that at the time of the expulsion each of these populations included fifty to sixty Jews who owned houses or land. In 1492 Mossé de Cuellar, a Jew from Buitrago, owned fifty-seven fields, eight orchards, twenty-four houses, a vineyard, three lots of land, and a granary with a place for washing wool and a cheese making facility. F. Cantera Burgos and C. Carrete Parrondo, "La judería de Buitrago," *Sefarad* 32 (1972): 3–87.

17. Documents on Juan Bravo and the Coronel family in L. F. de Peñalosa Archives, Segovia.

18. Pedro Corominas, *El sentimiento de la riqueza en Castilla* (Madrid: [Imp. de Fortanet], 1917).

19. Miguel Ángel Ladero Quesada, *El siglo XV en Castilla: fuentes de renta y política fiscal* (Barcelona: Ariel, 1982), pp. 154–55.

20. There were nevertheless examples of collective solidarity. The most famous was produced at the siege of Malaga in August 1487. The Jews who lived there, like its other inhabitants, were reduced to slavery when Christian troops entered the city. Their

ransom was fixed at 10 million maravedís, but the Jews of Malaga were only able to collect half that amount by selling their belongings (houses, furniture, and jewelry). In 1490 Abraham Seneor and his son-in-law Mayr Melamed offered the monarchs that the rest of the sum be covered by dividing the remainder among all the aljamas in Castile. The monarchs accepted the arrangement. Suárez Fernández, *La expulsión de los judíos,* vol. 1, p. 312.

21. Ibid., vol. 1, p. 272.

22. As of 1465 the construction of new synagogues had been prohibited.

23. There are a few odd and rare cases of Jews converting to Islam during this period. One such conversion occurred in the bishopric of Cartagena, another in Gualda-lajara. Upon a request made by the aljama of the latter city, the Royal Council decided in March of 1490 that such conversions would be prohibited.

24. In 1486 the Holy Brotherhood obliged Jews nevertheless to make contributions.

25. Due to a privilege obtained by Alfonso VIII in 1177 and confirmed in 1194 and 1305, the Moors and Jews of Palencia were under the bishop's jurisdiction. "They paid taxes and served the bishop and the Church of San Antolín."

26. Julio Caro Baroja, *Los judíos en la Espana moderna y contemporanea,* 3 vols. (Madrid: Ediciones Arion, 1961), vol. 2, p. 13.

27. In *Mélanges de la Casa de Velázquez* 11 (1975): 81–98, Jacqueline Buiral produced an investigation of the judicial records of the Valencian notary Jacques Salvador between 1474 and 1513 in which the names of 218 converts appeared. Eighty-seven had exercised professional occupations, forty-four were merchants, twenty-eight worked in the textile industry, and eight were shopkeepers. The tendency toward endogamy was very conspicuous; there were very few mixed marriages between converts and old Christians.

28. *Credere est voluntatis* [faith is a matter of free will]. The immense majority of sixteenth-century theologians and jurists maintained this principle against Sepúlveda, one that most notably inspired Bartolomé de las Casas.

29. M.-D. Chenu, "Orthodoxie et hérésie," *Annales, E.S.C.* (1963): 75–80.

30. This is how Lutherans in Vallodolid and Seville were qualified in 1559.

31. Angel Alcalá, "Juan de Lucena y el pre-Renacimiento español," *Revista Hispánica Moderna* 34 (1968): 120.

32. That is Henry Kamen's thesis in "Toleration and Dissent in Sixteenth-Century Spain: The Alternative Tradition," *Sixteenth Century Journal* 19 (1988): 7.

33. "The Jew turns his face to the wall in the hour of death, his body is washed with hot water, his beard is cut and shaven; the body is wrapped in new linen, a cushion filled with virgin earth is placed beneath the head and a coin or a pearl is placed in the mouth, water is run in the house." Charles Amiel, "'La mort juive' au regard des Inquisitions ibériques," *Revue d'histoire des religions* 4 (1990): 389–412.

34. Sometimes the inquisitors even came to aljamas to denounce converts who secretly practiced Judaism. A rabbi from Zaragoza, Rabbi Leví ben Sem Tob, presided in the synagogue three Saturdays, exhorting Jews of the aljama under threat of anathema to declare everything they knew about Christians who practiced Judaism in secret. Baer, *Historia de los judíos,* vol. 2, p. 602.

35. Eloy Benito Ruano, *Toledo en el siglo xv: Vida política* (Madrid: Consejo Superior de Investigaciones Científicas, Escuela de Estudios Medievales, 1961), p. 101.

36. Sebastián de Horozco, *Relaciones históricas toledanas,* edited by Jack Weiner (Toledo: I.P.I.E.T., 1981), p. 105. Perhaps this is the same case cited by Julio Caro Baroja (*Los judíos en la Espana,* vol. 3, p. 285) but attributed to Brother García Zapata, prior of the convent of the Geronimos of La Sisla, which every year in September celebrated the Feast of the Tabernacles in which a blessing at the moment of the Consecration begins, "Sus, periquete, que mira la gente¿" This is supposedly a reference to Jewish oratory during the Feast of the Tabernacles. The Spanish reads, "Sus, periquete, que os mira la gente¿"

37. The bones of Fernán Sánchez de Villanueva and his wife Elvira were unconverted and burned in Cuenca on September 29,1492. A. Coster, "Luis de León," *Revue Hispanique* 52 (1921): 28–29.

38. See, for example, Yolanda Moreno Coch, "La communidad judaizante de Castillo de Garcimuñoz, 1489–1492," *Sefarad* 37 (1977): 351–71.

39. "Basically the Inquisition's analysis of the converts' character was correct. . . .: they continued to be attached to the religion of their ancestors and their people and the majority observed Jewish rituals in secret or in public." Baer, *Historia de los judíos,* vol. 2, p. 639.

40. See I. S. Revah on this subject.

41. Julián Marías made this astute observation in *España inteligible: Razón histórica de las Españas* (Madrid: Alianza, 1985, p. 189), and I agree wholeheartedly with his explanation of this subject.

42. The same confusion between religious and cultural aspects was made regarding Moors in the sixteenth century: they dressed, ate, and amused themselves as did Muslims. The insinuation was that their beliefs were equally Islamic. After a hard day of labor in the field Moors would wash their feet in a "Moorish ceremony" as the old Christians interpreted the act.

43. Baer, *Historia de los judíos,* vol. 2, p. 527.

44. Ibid., vol. 2, p. 601. The inquisitorial trial of Alfonso de la Caballería was held in 1488 under the pope's direct supervision. It concluded in 1501 with the apostolic commission granting complete absolution.

45. Lucien Febvre, *Le problème de l'incroyance au XVIème siècle: La religion de Rabelais* (Paris: Albin Michel, 1962).

46. This phrase is found in a quotation in *Fortalitium fidei* by Brother Alonso de Espina (1460).

47. Robert Ricard, *"La Celestina* vista otra vez," in *Nouvelles études religieuses* (Paris: Centre de Recherches Hispaniques, 1973).

48. Note that in this entire debate no mention of the Islamic phenomenon is made, nor is there any reference to the Moors, who were, nevertheless, present in various areas of the peninsula. The issue of the presence of Muslims only began to become a serious one after the fall of Granada in 1492.

49. Oddly enough, the *Fortalium*'s unexpected influence can be observed in *De*

unico vocationis modo by Bartolomé de las Casas (Madrid: Alianza, 1990). That work aimed at expounding the Thomist doctrine of the conversion of infidels through persuasion and opposed that approach to the violence the Prophet Mohammed used to force people into submitting to Islamic domination. Las Casas cites the treatise by Alonso de Espina.

50. There were nevertheless exceptions such as, for example, the one made in 1479 through a petition to the General Council of the Holy Brotherhood in favor of its treasurer Abraham Seneor.

51. There were such cases. In 1485 the inquisitors of Córdoba harbored serious suspicions about Abraham Benveniste and his wife Oravida, accused of instigating converts to practice Judaism.

52. Ricardo García Cárcel, *Orígenes de la Inquisición española: El tribunal de Valencia, 1478–1530* (Barcelona: Peninsula, 1976), p. 38.

53. The term *inquisition* should be understood as an "in-depth investigation."

54. This included economic life. Kriegel notes the anti-Jewish hostility of traders, many of whom were converts, in Burgos and on the Cantabrian Coast ("La prise d'une décision," pp. 66–67).

55. "Today there is no doubt that the Inquisition was a satanical hispano-hebraic invention." Claudio Sánchez-Albornoz, *España: Un enigma histórico* (Buenos Aires: Editoral Sudamercana, 1956), vol. 2, p. 255.

56. In *Libro del Alborayque* a distinction is made between an *anusim* (a Jew who has been converted by force but secretly continues to be faithful to his belief) and a *mesumad* (sincerely converted). The *Alborayque* follows: "If some of this lineage arrives at some place where this bad generation is present, ask them, 'Are you anus, Christian by force, or mesumad, Christian by will?' If he responds, 'I am anus,' give him gifts and honor him and if he says, 'I am mesumad' do not speak to him any more."

57. *Codoin*, vol. 14, p. 372.

58. King Fernando declared much later in 1507, "We were told so many things in Andalusia that if they had said these things about our son, the prince [Don Juan, who died in 1497], we would have done the same to him."

59. Hernando de Talavera, *Católica impugnación* (Barcelona: Juan Flores, 1961), pp. 68–69. This was a piece of writing Talavera composed after 1481 in response to an anonymous tract by a crypto-Jew in Seville. The text has been reedited with a valuable introduction by Francisco Márquez Villanueva. Eugenio Asensio discovered a 1487 edition of the same (possibly the original). Talavera's work was included in the books indexed and prohibited by the General Inquisitor Valdés in 1559.

60. Talavera, *Católica impugnación*, pp. 150–51.

61. The Jews of those dioceses fled to Extremadura (Llerena, Jerez de los Caballeros, and Badajoz). By 1484 the Jewish community of Seville had disappeared. Was the expulsion order strictly applied? It seems that in 1485 there were still aljamas in Córdoba and Moguer (Tarsicio de Azcona, *Isabel la Católica*, pp. 640–41). In 1486 a similar expulsion of Jews occurred in Zaragoza and Teruel, but apparently it was not completely carried out as planned.

62. Hernando de Pulgar, *Crónica de los reyes Católicos*, edited by Juan de Mata Carriazo (Madrid: Espasa-Calpe, 1943), ch. 120.

63. Pulgar, *Crónica de los reyes Católicos*.

Chapter 5: The Expulsion

1. This document is in the Archives of the Kingdom of Aragon and was published in Rafael Conde y Delgado de Molina, *La expulsión de los judíos de la Corona de Aragón* (Zaragoza: Institutición Fernando el Católico, 1991), pp. 197–99.

2. This is the most widely known version. The original is in the Patronato Real section, General Archives of Simancas, Spain, leg. 28. ol. 6. See also *Boletín de la Real Academia de la Historia* 11 (1887): 512–28, and Luis Suárez Fernández, *Documentos acerca de la expulsión de los judíos* (Valladolid: n.p., 1964).

3. This document is conserved at the Archives of the Kingdom of Aragon, Barcelona, and is published in Conde y Delgado de Molina, *La expulsión*, pp. 41–44.

4. "Persuadiéndonos el venerable padre prior de Santa Cruz [Torquemada], inquisidor general de la dicha herética pravedad."

5. Mention is made of the "abominable" circumcisions and "Jewish perfidy." Moreover, Judaism is qualified as "leprosy," expressions that are not included in the Castilian version.

6. "We find these Jews to have committed rampant and intolerable acts of usury, thus devouring and absorbing the food and shelter of Christians." I do not agree with Conde, for whom the Aragonese decree is more sober in terms of religious accusations (Conde y Delgado de Molina, *La expulsión*, p. 10). These are the same as those of the other two versions but aggravated by the use of much more injurious language.

7. He proposed a great sum of money to Don Fernando. The story goes that upon hearing of this proposition Torquemada went before the king and placed a cross at his feet, exclaiming in a dramatic manner, "Judas sold Our Lord for 30 silver pieces and His Majesty is about to sell it again for 30,000."

8. In a work written in the mid-sixteenth century there is a passage concerning the era of the Catholic monarchs: "Most of the Jews and Moors who converted to our holy Catholic faith took as their baptismal godfathers the most prominent noblemen [*hidalgos*] and gentlemen [*caballeros*] of the places where they were baptized and honored them by taking their last names. They thus came under their protection and got along so well with them that they were introduced and designated as one of their own, especially where they were not known [previously]." Diego de Hermosilla, *Diálogo de los pajes*, edited by Donald MacKenzie (Valladolid: Widow of Montero, 1916), p. 60.

9. Yitzhak Baer, *Historia de los judíos en la España cristiana*, translated by Jose Luis Lacave, 2 vols. (Madrid: Altalena, 1981), vol. 2, p. 648.

10. Born in Lisbon in 1437 and an intimate friend of the Braganza family, whose relations with the Portuguese dynasty were not very good, he had to go to Toledo in 1483. A short time later he entered the Catholic monarchs' service as a financier. A politician and immensely rich philanthropist as well as a Bible scholar who was proud of his

lineage and even claimed to be a descendant of King David, he was not convinced by the Catholic monarchs and fled to Italy. He died in Padova in 1508 at seventy. His son Judah, better known as Leon the Hebrew, wrote the famous love dialogs (*Dialoghi di amore*) inspired by Plato.

11. Quoted by Antonio Domínguez Ortiz, *La clase social de los conversos en Castilla en la Edad Modern* (Granada: University of Granada, 1991), pp. 27–28.

12. Andrés Bernáldez, *Memorias del reinado de los reyes Católicos*, edited by Manuel Gómez-Moreno and Juan de Mata Carriazo (Madrid: Blass S.A. Tipográfica, 1962), chs. 110–11.

13. Baer, *Historia de los judíos,* vol. 2, p. 648.

14. Domínguez Ortiz, *La clase social*, pp. 27–28.

15. The city of Vitoria faithfully kept this promise a secret until it was revealed in 1952 by the Jewish community of Bayonne. That occurred during a post–World War II ceremony in recognition of the safe haven given descendents of the Jews expelled in 1492 who were escaping Nazi persecution.

16. For example, Martín de Gurrea, lord of Argovieso, was responsible for the protection of Aragonese Jews. Conde y Delgado de Molina, *La expulsión,* p. 33.

17. Francisco del Aguila says that he converted with fifty-three people, Galfón Falcó claimed that "many" came with him, Juan Pérez de la Concha was accompanied by five people, and Juan de Vargas was baptized along with his wife and nine sons and their maid. Luis Suárez Fernández, *La expulsión de los judíos de España* (Madrid: Editorial MAPFRE, 1991), vol. 2, p. 342.

18. Decree dated August 6, 1499, in Granada. Cited by Juan Meseguer Fernández in the collective work published as *La Inquisición española,* edited by Joaquín Pérez (Villanueva Madrid, n.d.), pp. 376–79.

19. Suárez Fernández, *La expulsión de los judíos,* vol. 2, p. 343.

20. A Jewish chronicle from the sixteenth century recounts the adventure as follows: "They embarked confidently and went on their way. When they were en route, the sailors then rose up against them, took their belongings from them, attached them with chords, insulted their wives as soon as they saw them, and were left with no one who could save them from that day of divine fury." Yosef ha-Kohen, *'Emeq ha-Bakha* (The Valley of Tears), trans. and ann. by Pilar León Tello (Madrid: Consejo Superior de Investigaciones Científicas, Instituto Arias Montano, 1964), pp. 181–82. The son of expelled Spaniards, Yosef ha-Kohen was born on French soil and later settled in Italy as a doctor.

21. Domínguez Ortiz, *La clase social*, p. 30n.

22. Francisco López de Gomara, *Anales del emperador Carlos V,* edited and translated by Roger Bigelow Merriman (New York: Oxford University Press, 1912).

23. "We are astonished that you think that we want to take for Ourselves possessions belonging to the Jews, because it is something very distant from Our wishes. . . . Although we want our Court to recover, as is reasonable, all that rightfully belongs to it of these belongings, that is, debts owed to us by these Jews due in taxes or other royal rents

that we have over this aljama; but, once paid what is owed Us and owed to creditors, what remains should be returned to the Jews, to each one according to what belongs to him, so that they may do with it what they want." King Fernando to the Governor of Aragon, June 11, 1492, in Conde y Delgado de Molina, *La expulsión,* pp. 95–96.

24. Carriazo observes that in approximately 1480–82 the emigration of converts from Seville to seigneurial country domains caused a veritable collapse in the city's commerce and in royal rents collected. He cites a petition by the overseer (*mayordomo*) Juan de Sevilla dated September 2, 1482: "The aforementioned converts were the main tax collectors." Their departure provoked a great decline in municipal finances. Juan de Mata Carriazo, "La Inquisición y las rentas de Sevilla," in *Homenaje a D. Ramón Carande,* 2 vols. (Madrid: Sociedad de Estudios y Publicaciones, 1963), vol. 2, pp. 95–112.

25. King Fernando's response to the city of Barcelona was, "Before having deliberated about having an Inquisition take place in any city in our kingdom, we considered and [fore]saw all the costs and increases that might follow and would come out of our rights and royal rents. But as our firm intention in this is to prefer serving our Lord our God. . . . we want it to be done in any case, all other interests being deferred." Baer, *Historia de los judíos,* vol. 2, p. 609. Queen Isabel is attributed with the same idea, almost in the same terms: "As it was desired that the absence of these people depopulate a good part of the city [of Seville], the Queen was informed that the great commerce that she had in it would diminish and for this reason her rents would be significantly lowered, but she esteemed that the decrease in her rents was of little importance and said that, all interest deferred, she wanted to cleanse her kingdom of this sin of heresy." Hernando de Pulgar, *Crónica de los Reyes Católicos,* edited by Juan de Mata Carriazo (Madrid: Epasa-Calpe, 1943), ch. 120.

26. The history of the former Soviet Union is a noteworthy example. Its leaders well knew that their politics of liquidating the free countryside and establishing a state-controlled economy would provoke immediate chaos prejudicial to the development of production. Nevertheless, they for ages maintained a strict policy because they were more interested in building a new type of society based on collectivism. In this case they sacrificed economic productivity and benefits to an ideology. Raymond Aron writes that "[the Soviet leaders] subordinate economic rationality to ideological rationality; or rather, if one prefers another expression, they prefer ideology to economy, the dogma of collective property over the individualistic spirit, linked to private property." Aron, *Plaidoyer pour l'Europe décadente* (Paris: R. Laffont, 1977), p. 85.

27. "Is it inconsiderate to think that, once again, in a country overpopulated in terms of its resources, and this was the case of the Iberian peninsula during the reign of the Catholic Monarchs, that religion was the pretext as much as the cause for persecution and emigration?" Fernand Braudel, *La Méditerranée et le monde méditerranéen à l'époque de Phillippe II,* 2 vols. (Paris: Hachette, 1966), vol. 1, p. 380.

28. Henry Kamen, *La inquisición española,* 3d ed., rev. and exp. (Barcelona: Crítica, 1988).

29. This is also the thesis defended some years ago by A. J. Saraiva in *A inquisição portuguesa* (Lisbon: Europa-América, 1956) and in *Inquisição e cristiãos-novos* (Porto: Edi-

torial Inova, 1969) and B. Netanyahu, *The Marranos of Spain from the Late Fourteenth to the Early Sixteenth Century* (New York: New York Academy for Jewish Research, 1966). Religion simply masked class struggle. It was not so much the eradication of Judaism that was achieved as the elimination of *Marranos* (crypto-Jews) because in reality the immense majority of converts were sincere Christians. Paradoxically, it was the Inquisition that renewed Marranism. I. S. Revah, who was very knowledgeable about peninsular Marranism, was opposed to this interpretation: "If all the new Christians had been persecuted without real religious motives, we could not explain the millions fled from the sixteenth to the eighteenth centuries to join Jewish communities or found new ones in countries where Judaism was previously unofficially tolerated, publicly allowed or sometimes totally unknown." Revah, "Les marranes portugais et l'Inquisition au XVIᵉ siècle," in *Etudes portugaises*, ed. Charles Amiel (Paris, 1975): 185–228.

30. According to what exiled Jews said in 1492, the expulsion had displeased the magnates. Suárez Fernández, *La expulsión de los judíos*, p. 259.

31. S. H. Haliczer, "The Castilian Urban Patriciate and the Jewish Expulsions of 1480–1492," *American Historical Review* 78 (1973): 35–58.

32. J. M. Monsalvo Antón, *Teoría y evolución de un conflicto social: El antisemitismo en la Corona de Castilla en la Baja Edad Media* (Madrid: Siglo Veintiuno, 1985), p. 91.

33. Isabel, with waning hopes of obtaining a male successor to the throne, called upon a Jewish doctor, Lorenzo Badoz, whose treatment then led to the birth of Prince Don Juan.

34. This opinion is shared by some Jewish sources who hold King Fernando mainly responsible for the expulsion decree. Tarsicio de Azcona, *Isabel la Católica* (Madrid: Biblioteca de Autores Cristianos, 1993), p. 645.

35. Joseph Pérez, *Isabelle et Ferdinand, rois catholiques d'Espagne* (Paris: Fayard, 1988), ch. 4.

36. "Hallamos los dichos judíos, por medio de grandísimas e insoportables usuras, devorar y absorber las haciendas y sustancias de los cristianos, ejerciendo inicuamente y sin piedad la pravedad usuraria contra los dichos cristianos públicamente y manifiesta como contra enemigos y reputándolos idólatras, de lo cual graves querellas de nuestros súbditos y naturales a nuestras orejas han pervenido." [We find the aforementioned Jews, by way of great and intolerable usury, to have devoured and absorbed the properties and means of Christians, iniquitously and pitilessly exercising usurious depravity against these Christians, publicly manifest as against enemies and reputing them as idolaters, [due to] which our subjects and citizens have had serious disputes which have come to our attention.]

37. This was true in spite of the very recent case of the Holy Infant of La Guardia, concluded only four months before the signing of the decree.

38. This is the position that Luis Suárez Fernández has always defended: "The Monarchs clearly distinguished between ideas and people: they attempted to eliminate once and for all Judaism as a tolerated religious doctrine" (*Historia de España, edad media* [Madrid: Editorial Gredos, 1970], vol. 17–2, p. 241). More recently, Miguel Ángel Ladero Quesada has also asserted the same idea with similar reasoning: "The main

objective. . . . was not to attack those whose blood was of the Jewish nation, but rather to indicate to many of its members they indirectly encouraged the phenomena of xenophobia, unless they eradicated Judaism as a religious faith" (*Historia 16,* no. 194).

39. It is most especially Isabel who was taxed with this label whereas Fernando, perhaps due to the influence of Machiavelli's opinions, was attributed with much more rational motivations: using religion for political ends. Nevertheless, J. A. Llorente in *A History of the Inquisition of Spain* (London: G. B. Whittaker, 1827; repr. Madrid: Hiperión, 1980), attributes the creation of the Holy Office to King Fernando, who was much more enthusiastic than the queen in this matter.

40. "A legend circulated among Jews according to which Fernando or Isabel, or both, would have made a sacred promise, almost a vow, of expelling the Jews if God helped them to eliminate the kingdom of Granada." Suárez Fernández, *La expulsión de los judíos,* p. 319.

41. [Pope Alexander VI (1431–1503), a Spaniard named Rodrigo Borgia, was the nephew of Pope Callistus III (1378–1458). When Borgia became pope in 1492 it was through bribery and literal nepotism. His main interests during his pontificate were political and familial—notably the promotion of his illegitimate son, Caesar Borgia (1475–1507), Machiavellli's prince. Alexander VI was responsible for dividing the New World between Portugal and Spain; the crusade against the Moors; and the trial, torture, and execution of Girolamo Savonarola, the Dominican reformer. A corrupt ruler known to have led an immoral life, it appears that his only saving grace was his patronage of the arts (i.e., Bramante). The Borgia clan epitomizes some of the worst enmeshed church and state politics in European history.]

42. This said, I do not ignore the religious dimension of each of these events. The concept of crusade in the war of Granada, the desire to expand and extol the faith, the Messianic and providentialist exaltation, and the millenary spirit of the period. What I do want to posit is that political preoccupations ultimately inspired the sovereigns' actions, despite and beyond that dimension.

43. And for some converts? A Jewish chronicle, written a short time after 1492, accuses the convert Alfonso de la Caballería of having inspired the monarchs with the idea of expulsion. In 1503 another convert, Juan de Lucena, asked for King Fernando's protection in a matter pending before the Inquisition in Zaragoza in which some Jews had intervened "as our enemies. . . . , because of their expulsion, which they blame me for entirely" (Llorente, *Historia crítica de la Inquisición*). I thank Maurice Kriegel for having allowed me to read "Entre 'question' des nouveaux-Chrétiens et expulsion des Juifs," in *Xudeus e Conversos na Historia,* edited by Carlos Barros (Santiago de Compostela: La Editorial de la Historia, 1994), in which he comments on these facts. Kriegel sustains that this is yet another example of the aversion of some Jews for converts who had abandoned Judaism for Christianity under conditions considered indecent at the end of the fourteenth and beginning of the fifteenth centuries.

44. Kriegel, "Entre 'question' des nouveaux-Chrétiens."

45. Julián Marías, *España inteligible* (Madrid: Alianza, 1985), p. 183.

46. France is a curious case. The Catholic masses obliged King Henry IV to renounce to Protestantism not the reverse. Indeed, "Paris is well worth a mass!"

47. Nor was Catholicism for that matter.

48. Maurice Kriegel, *Les Juifs à la fin du Moyen Age dans l'Europe méditerranéenne* (Paris: Hachette, 1979).

49. Insertion or integration? "Integration leaves whole the problem of the religious specificity of Islam and the forms of its expression in the framework of a secular republic. . . . In the logic of integration, pushed to its extreme limits, any sign of affirmation of the Islamic identity would be a hint of the refusal to accept the privatization of the religious believer. . . . The logic of insertion implies that within the society welcoming foreigners, a separate identity remains that erects certain ethno-cultural particularities into binding legal criteria aimed at avoiding the dissolution of the community entity and the dispersion, through integration and then through assimilation, of the individuals composing it." G. Kepel in *La France dans deux générations: population et société dans le premier tiers du XXIe siècle*, edited by Georges Tapinos et al. (Paris: Fayard, 1992), pp. 291–92.

50. Then as now, reference is made to the odor of certain groups of immigrants. Today, the expulsion of foreigners takes place via special charter flights. What were the boats requisitioned in Cádiz and other ports for the departure of Spanish Jews if not *charters avant la lettre*?

Epilogue

1. *El País*, March 26, 1992.

2. Américo Castro, *Lo hispánico y el erasmismo: Los prólogos al "Quijote"* (Buenos Aires: Facultad de filosofía y letras de la Universidad de Buenos Aires, 1942).

3. Only Vauban (in 1689) regretted the damage this measure had inflicted upon the kingdom.

Appendix

1. Archives of the Kingdom of Aragon and published in Rafael Conde y Delgado de Molina, *La expulsión de los judíos de la Corona de Aragón* (Zaragoza: Institutición Fernando el Católico, 1991), pp. 197–99.

2. Don Enrique de Aragon y Pimentel, the Count of Ampurias, Duke of Segorbia, and King Fernando's cousin, was named delegate in charge in Catalonia on November 11, 1479.

3. [The Church used the Latin term to designate the inquisitors' target was *pravitas heretica* (heretical depravity). The concept of heresy was an expanding one—indeed, it was spreading like any disease that gets a name by those who seek to diagnose and treat it. The Inquisition (the Church, pope, inquisitors, and ultimately the Catholic monarchs) defined and redefined the crime, thus expanding the jurisdiction of the Inquisition, which had run its course in the rest of Europe when it was revived in

Spain. See "Inquisition: Middle Ages" and "Inquisition: Modern Period," *Dictionary of the History of the Papacy* (New York: Routledge, 2002).]

4. *Portantveus: lugarteniente:* lieutenant, delegate, deputy.

5. *Paeres: regidores:* aldermen, governors.

6. Here the word refers to the "new Christians" or *cristianos nuevos*.

7. The Spanish word is *ayuntamiento*, which refers to local governing bodies and the places where the governing takes place. In this context the translation of "congregation" should be extended to take on a larger sense to include a union, joint; corporation or body of magistrates in cities or towns; municipal government; and townhall, guildhall, or guild organization descriptive of the Jews' collective autonomous and separate judicial, administrative, and religious practices within and beyond the aljama structures. *Cassell's Spanish-English, English Spanish Dictionary* and *Funk and Wagnalls,* 1960 and subsequent editions.

8. *Guerrea ligeramente:* "wars lightly" (lit.)

9. This new deadline added nine days, extending the final date for expulsion to July 31. Although the extension was not mentioned in the two royal edicts dated March 31, it was, in fact, the deadline that was applied in 1492.

10. Decree for the Kingdom of Castile. Patronato Real section, General Archives of Simancas, Spain, leg. 28. ol. 6; Luis Suárez Fernández, *Documentos acerca de la expulsión de los judíos* (Valladolid: n.p., 1964).

11. To "judaize" is to practice Judaism, understood as a form of crypto-Judaism, because such practices by Christians (i.e., false converts) were condemned by the Inquisition, which in effect enforced conversions.

12. For *Cristianos* see note 6.

13. *Colegio y universidad:* any collective body.

14. [Fernando and Isabel adopted precisely the language used by Torquemada to justify the collective expulsion of the Jews and false converts. The term *university* and the advent of the first European universities in the twelfth and thirteenth centuries were based on the concept borrowed from peninsular Arab philosophy, especially the philosophy of Averroes Cordubensis (Abu Walid Ibn Rochd). In the latter half of the thirteenth century Arab philosophy in the form of Averroism and the teaching of Aristotle was condemned and forbidden in European universities such as the Sorbonne. Perhaps this is the precedent referred to in the edicts. Otherwise the term has rather wide usage in the period preceding the edicts. "*Universitas* is synonymous of *Res publica*. It then means the most concrete of assemblies—the *universitas* of bakers, doctors, grammarians . . . (*Hostiensis*) or the most abstract—the *universitas* of philosophers, that of the human race, that of citizens, that of the people of Israel, either dispersed or reunited in Herod's kingdom (in Hilaire de Poitiers). The *universitas* of causes, the *universitas* of forms, in Avicenna—Ibn Sin—or in Ibn Gabirol, in Gundisalvi's translations, that of monasteries in Bernard de Clairvaux." Jean-Pierre Faye, "Le sujet dans la nuit mouvante: Résonance Averroiste en Europe," in *Le Métis Culturel* (Paris: Maison des Cultures du Monde, 1994), p. 62. In turn, the revival of

ancient Roman law meant that res publica was a key concept in the papal justification of the jurisprudence of the Inquisition held for the public's well-being.]

15. Archives of the Kingdom of Aragon and published in Rafael Conde y Delgado de Molina, *La expulsión de los judíos de la Corona de Aragón* (Zaragoza: Institución Fernando el Católico, 1991), pp. 41–44.

16. For *Christians* see note 6.

17. For *colegio o universidad* see note 13.

Index

Index

Index

Index

Index

Index

JOSEPH PÉREZ is the author of such publications as *La révolution des "Communidades" de Castille, 1520–1521* (1970), *Isabelle et Ferdinand: Rois Catholiques d'Espagne* (1988), *Carlos V* (2004), and *The Spanish Inquisition: A History* (2005). He is emeritus professor of history at the University of Bordeaux and honorary director of the Casa de Velazquez in Madrid.

LYSA HOCHROTH is publications editor with the International Council of Museums. She has also taught at Columbia University, American University, and the University of the District of Columbia and translated numerous other works.

HELEN NADER is professor of history at the University of Arizona; author of *The Mendoza Family in the Spanish Renaissance* and *Liberty in Absolutist Spain: The Habsburg Sale of Towns;* and editor and translator of *Power and Gender in Renaissance Spain: Eight Women of the Mendoza Family* and *The Book of Privileges Issued to Christopher Columbus by King Fernando and Queen Isabel.*

~ Hispanisms

The University of Illinois Press
is a founding member of the
Association of American University Presses.

———————————————————————

Composed in 10.5/13 Minion
with Caflish display and Arabesque Ornaments
by Type One, LLC
for the University of Illinois Press
Designed by Dennis Roberts
Manufactured by Thomson-Shore, Inc.

University of Illinois Press
1325 South Oak Street
Champaign, IL 61820-6903
www.press.uillinois.edu